THE DEGOLYER LIBRARY

PUBLICATION SERIES

VOLUME TWO

# Ten Days on the Plains

By Henry E. Davies

EDITED BY

PAUL ANDREW HUTTON

THE DEGOLYER LIBRARY

SOUTHERN METHODIST UNIVERSITY PRESS

DALLAS

LIBRARY OF CONGRESS CATALOGUING-IN-PUBLICATION DATA

Davies, Henry Eugene, 1836-1894.
Ten days on the plains.

(DeGolyer library publication series; v. 2)
Reprint. Originally published: New York: Printed
by Crocker & Co., 1871.
Includes index.
1. West (U.S.)—Description and travel—1860-1880.
2. Bill, Buffalo, 1846-1917. 3. Hunting—West (U.S.)—
History—19th century. 4. Buffalo—History—19th
century. 5. Davies, Henry Eugene, 1836-1894—Journeys—
West (U.S.) I. Hutton, Paul Andrew, 1949-   . II. Title. III. Series.
F594.D25 1985     917.8'042     85-10915
ISBN 0-87074-207-8

FRONTISPIECE: William F. "Buffalo Bill" Cody poses with three unidentified friends
in this tintype image from the late 1860s. Cody balances his .50-caliber Springfield
buffalo-hunting rifle, Lucretia Borgia, across his knee.

DESIGNED BY LAURY A. EGAN

To

ROBERT M. UTLEY

# CONTENTS

# List of Illustrations

FACSIMILE ILLUSTRATIONS

# FOREWORD

AS a first-person account of a military sponsored hunting expedition to the plains, Henry Eugene Davies' *Ten Days on the Plains* stands, if perhaps unintentionally, at a pivotal point in the history of the American West. As Paul A. Hutton notes in his fine introduction to this reprint of the original account, Davies captures William F. "Buffalo Bill" Cody at the moment of his transition from a well-respected frontier scout to showman, and, simultaneously, Davies captures the emergence of the West itself into myth.

Due in no small part to "Buffalo Bill's Wild West," the image of the West became indelibly linked in people's minds with the romanticism of cowboys, rustlers, wild Indians, and saloons. It is unlikely that Davies, in focusing so much of his account upon Cody, appreciated just to what extent he was helping to create the western myth; after all, he published his account privately and did so for only the members of the expedition. It is also unlikely that he understood the significance of the buffalo hunt that he so effectively described. His companions may have thrilled at the easy slaughter of the buffalo, but, if unwittingly, they did much to publicize and justify Major General Philip Sheridan's strategy of attrition against the plains Indians, a policy that, as Paul Hutton notes, Grant, Sherman, and Sheridan first employed so effectively against the Confederacy only a few years before. It is ironic that an account that glorifies the romantic myth of the West also underscores the crass elimination of the food supply of the free-roaming tribes of the plains, insuring their eventual defeat.

Davies' *Ten Days on the Plains* is thus a fascinating account which in several different ways catches the plains area at a crossroads in its development. Following the year of the expedition, change was, of course, dramatic. Still, it is difficult today to appreciate fully just how different the West in 1871 was from what it had been only a few years earlier. Parkman's *The Oregon Trail*, like many other earlier accounts, gives a much different impression of the region than Davies' account does. That Davies and his party actually enjoyed their trek into an area that to earlier travellers had been a dry, desolate wilderness speaks clearly to just how much the plains had already changed by 1871. *Ten Days on the Plains* is an entertaining portrayal of the West in transition; it is here that Davies' account achieves its importance.

In publishing *Ten Days on the Plains* with the SMU Press, the DeGolyer Library is making available a previously little known, but nonetheless vivid and important, western travel account. The account is published in facsimile from the pages of the original document. Everette Lee DeGolyer, Sr., the geologist, oil entrepreneur, and bookman, originally purchased the title for his private collection, years prior to the establishment of the DeGolyer Library at Southern Methodist University. Today, the DeGolyer Library's copy of *Ten Days on the Plains* is one of the library's most fascinating titles in its 55,000-volume Western History Collection. The copy is one of several copies known to exist today. In reprinting the book, the library aims to make more readily available what is an exceedingly scarce historical account. The facsimile is strongly complemented by Hutton's notes and introduction. Hutton carefully explores several themes suggested by the account, focusing primarily on Cody and the development of the western myth.

Henry Eugene Davies' *Ten Days on the Plains* is the second title to be issued in the DeGolyer Library Publication Series, joining David J. Weber's *Troubles in Texas, 1832: A Tejano Viewpoint from San Antonio*, which the library published in 1983.

CLIFTON H. JONES
DIRECTOR

*DeGolyer Library*
*Fikes Hall of Special Collections*
*May 1985*

# ACKNOWLEDGMENTS

MANY PEOPLE assisted in the publication of this book, and it is a particular pleasure to acknowledge their contributions. David J. Weber, chairman of the history department at Southern Methodist University and editor of the first volume in this series, suggested the topic and offered timely advice and encouragement.

Clifton H. Jones, former director of Fikes Hall of Special Collections and the DeGolyer Library, assisted with some of the research for this book. He and his fine staff were most helpful and a delight to work with.

Paul Fees, curator of the Buffalo Bill Museum, Buffalo Bill Historical Center, Cody, Wyoming, provided research materials and suggested illustrations for the book. He also located the unpublished early photograph of Buffalo Bill Cody used as this book's frontispiece and secured permission from the Garlow family for its publication. The editor and publisher acknowledge the kindness of the Garlow family in allowing the publication of the photograph.

Constance K. Mohrman, curator at the Museum of Western Art, Denver, was most helpful in locating illustrations for *Ten Days on the Plains*. She also provided the dust jacket illustration and information on its artist.

Assistance with illustrations was provided by Stanley W. Zamonski, curator of the Buffalo Bill Memorial Museum, Golden, Colorado; Elaine Eatroff, rare book curator at the United States Military Academy Library; Shari Small of the Buffalo Bill Historical Center; Dawn Letson of the DeGolyer Library; Art DeBacker of the Kansas State Historical Society; and John Carter of the Nebraska State Historical Society.

Thanks are also due David Miller and Cal Fastwolf of the Center for the History of the American Indian, Newberry Library,

S. Douglas Youngkin, Raymond J. DeMallie, D. Teddy Diggs, Trudy McMurrin, and Paul Hedren.

Volume One in the DeGolyer Library Publication Series was dedicated to Everett Lee DeGolyer, Jr., and Lon Tinkle, both long associated with Southern Methodist University and the library. This second volume in the series is dedicated to Robert M. Utley. As the dean of historians of the military frontier, Utley has set the standards for this field of scholarship. His dedication to writing sound, readable history for laymen as well as scholars, his generosity of spirit in assisting younger historians, and his high standards of scholarship have marked him as one of the preeminent historians of the American frontier.

PAUL ANDREW HUTTON

*University of New Mexico*
*Albuquerque, New Mexico*

# Ten Days on the Plains

# INTRODUCTION

𝇋

W HEN Henry Eugene Davies wrote *Ten Days on the Plains* he probably never dreamed that it would be read by many more people than his companions on the hunting expedition that the book chronicles. It was privately printed in 1872 in an extremely limited edition, and a copy was sent to each participant in the hunt. In time it became one of the rarest items of western Americana, with fine copies selling for over $1,500.

The book is as delightful to read as it is hard to find. It has intrinsic value as a narrative of the western buffalo country in 1871. Covering almost two hundred miles in ten days, Davies and his companions left a trail of empty champagne bottles and animal carcasses from Fort McPherson, Nebraska, to Fort Hays, Kansas. Over six hundred buffalo were slaughtered, along with hundreds of elk, antelope, and wild turkeys before the junket was over. Frontier luminaries like William F. "Buffalo Bill" Cody, Lieutenant General Philip Henry Sheridan, and Major Eugene Carr added considerable color to the enterprise. That alone justifies reprinting the little volume for a wider audience. There is more to the book, however, than its charm as a travel narrative. Although Davies scarcely intended it to do so, the book touches on three interesting themes in frontier history. First, it displays the close working relationship between the frontier military and the business community in the opening and exploitation of the West. Although the trip that Davies writes about was one of the largest of its type, it was hardly the only one.

Second, the book describes the wanton slaughter of western wildlife and unconsciously exposes the part played by the army in this environmental disaster. Many army officers were avid sportsmen, but the incredible destruction of life represented by this expedition went beyond sport. General Sheridan, the host of this hunting party, had initiated a policy of exterminating the buffalo as a way of destroying the economic base of the plains Indians. This hunting junket, and others like it, aided him in this cause.

Third, the book captures one of the most interesting and important frontier heroes, Buffalo Bill Cody, at almost the exact moment of his transition from authentic frontier scout and guide to romantic showman. Since Cody eventually emerged as the single most important hero of the post–Civil War frontier, the book takes on added importance as a contribution to the study of the evolution of an American hero.

We can be sure that the author had no intention in writing this volume other than to provide a memento of a delightful excursion for his companions. Davies, like the other members of the hunting party, was a member in good standing in the highest circles of northern, Gilded Age society. He also had an impressive military record and counted General Sheridan among his best friends. Born in New York City on July 2, 1836, the eldest son of a distinguished jurist, Davies was educated at Harvard and Columbia College. After studying law he was admitted to the bar but had barely begun his practice when the Civil War broke out in 1861. He entered the volunteer forces soon after the attack on Fort Sumter as a captain in the Fifth Regiment, New York Infantry. Later that year he was appointed major of the Second New York Cavalry and within two years became that regiment's colonel. Promoted to brigadier general in September 1863, Davies commanded first a brigade and then a division of the Army of the Potomac's Cavalry Corps. He accompanied General Sheridan as a division commander in the 1864 Shenandoah Valley campaign, distinguishing himself repeatedly in hard fighting. He was wounded at Hatcher's Run, Virginia, on February 6, 1865, in the campaign that led to Lee's surrender at Appomattox two months later. In recognition of this fine record he was promoted to major general of volunteers on May 4, 1865.[1]

Davies resigned from the army in January 1866 and returned to his law practice, but he never forgot his military associations. He was an early member of the New York Commandery of the Loyal Legion, an important Union veterans' organization. When the pub-

---

[1] For Henry E. Davies' military career see Francis B. Heitman, *Historical Register and Dictionary of the United States Army*, 2 vols. (Washington, D.C.: Government Printing Office, 1903), 1: 356; Ezra J. Warner, *Generals in Blue: Lives of the Union Commanders* (Baton Rouge: Louisiana State University Press, 1964), 113; and Stephen Z. Starr, *The Union Cavalry in the Civil War: The War in the East from Gettysburg to Appomattox 1863–1865* (Baton Rouge: Louisiana State University Press, 1981).

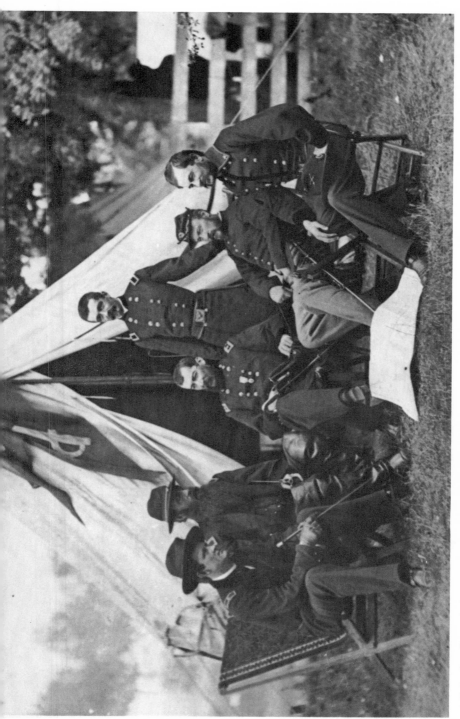

1. Brigadier General Henry E. Davies stands behind his commander, Major General Philip H. Sheridan, in this Brady and Company photograph taken at Lighthouse Point (Jordan's Point), near City Point, Virginia, in July 1864. Sheridan and Davies were soon to depart for the Shenandoah Valley campaign. Left to right: Brigadier General Wesley Merritt, Brigadier General David McMurtrie Gregg, Sheridan, Davies, Brigadier General James H. Wilson, and Brigadier General Alfred T. A. Torbert.

lishing firm of D. Appleton and Company initiated its distinguished "Great Commanders" series, the editor, J. G. Wilson, enlisted Davies to write the volume on Sheridan.[2]

From 1866 until 1869 Davies served as public administrator of New York City, and as assistant district attorney general of the southern district of New York from 1870 to 1872. He eventually retired from his successful law practice to the family home at Fishkill-on-the-Hudson, New York. He died on September 7, 1894, and was buried at St. Luke's Church, not far from his home.

Davies' Civil War commander, Lieutenant General Philip Henry Sheridan, hosted the hunting expedition. Sheridan had emerged from the war as the junior member of the trinity of great Union commanders. His rise to fame and high command, however, was more rapid and surprising than that of either of his good friends Ulysses S. Grant or William T. Sherman.

Born in Albany, New York, on March 6, 1831, Sheridan was raised in Somerset, Ohio, where his family moved while his father worked as a laborer on a road construction crew. Despite his Irish-Catholic origins, which normally would have led him to vote Democratic, Sheridan's father had strong Whig political connections and used them to get his son appointed to the United States Military Academy at West Point. A fight with another cadet delayed young Sheridan's graduation by one year, but he managed to graduate from West Point in 1853 despite low grades and a high number of conduct demerits.

The pugnacious shavetail served on the Indian frontier in Texas and Oregon, winning recognition from his superiors as a scrappy, intelligent combat officer. The attack on Fort Sumter found Sheridan a thirty-year-old captain of infantry, but thereafter his rise in rank was meteoric. Sheridan was optimistic concerning his chances for success, confiding to a friend that if the war lasted long enough he hoped to "have a chance to earn a major's commission."[3]

After commanding a desk as chief quartermaster for General Samuel R. Curtis's Army of the Southwest, headquartered in Missouri, Sheridan gained an appointment as colonel of the Second Michigan Cavalry. He was promoted to brigadier general of volunteers in September 1862 and quickly won a high reputation in

---

[2] Henry E. Davies, *General Sheridan* (New York: D. Appleton and Company, 1895). Davies also authored a geneological and biographical guide to his family, published in 1895, and a monograph on the New York City system of taxation, published in 1883.

[3] Whitelaw Reid, *Ohio in the War: Her Statesmen, Her Generals, and Soldiers*, 2 vols. (New York: Moore, Wilstach and Baldwin, 1868), 1: 500.

army circles for tenacity and courage by his actions at Perryville, Kentucky, and Stone's River, Tennessee.

Sheridan's counterattack at Stone's River turned seeming defeat into an important but grisly Union victory and earned him a second star in the volunteer army. It was his bold charge up Missionary Ridge, however, that secured General Ulysses S. Grant's esteem and guaranteed his future. Sheridan had shared in the humiliation of the Army of the Cumberland, first defeated at Chickamauga, Georgia, and then besieged in Chattanooga, Tennessee. When, on November 25, 1863, Sheridan's Second Division was given a chance at redemption they did not waste it.

Sheridan's men easily took the rifle pits at the base of Missionary Ridge, as ordered by Grant, but then faced a murderous fire from the seemingly impregnable Confederate positions on the crest of the ridge, four hundred feet above them. To advance up the ridge seemed suicidal, but it was equally dangerous to stay in the rifle pits.

Sheridan, taking out a pewter flask that he always carried, toasted the Confederate headquarters directly above him and gulped down the brandy. A thunderous rebel volley answered his impertinence, sending dirt and rock flying all around the bantam general. Cursing loudly, Sheridan tossed the flask up the ridge, mounted his black charger Rienzi, and led his division roaring up Missionary Ridge.

The press would later call it the miracle at Missionary Ridge. The Army of the Cumberland, with Sheridan's division leading, swept up the ridge to plant their regimental colors on the crest. Sheridan, unlike the other Union commanders, did not halt after taking the summit but plunged after the retreating rebels.

General Grant, who had watched the assault, was delighted. "Sheridan showed his genius in that battle," Grant later declared, "and to him I owe the capture of most of the prisoners that were taken. Although commanding a division only, he saw in the crisis of that engagement that it was necessary to advance beyond the point indicated by his orders. He saw what I could not know, on account of my ignorance of the ground, and with the instinct of military genius pushed ahead."[4]

When Grant, now in command of all Union forces, went east in March 1864 he took Sheridan with him to command the Army of the Potomac's cavalry. Sheridan soon led his ten thousand troopers on a bold raid to the very gates of Richmond, brushing aside the

[4] Bruce Catton, *Grant Takes Command* (Boston: Little, Brown and Company, 1968), 90.

vaunted rebel cavalry along the way and killing the Confederate cavalry commander, J.E.B. Stuart, at Yellow Tavern.

Grant rewarded Sheridan with an independent command in the Shenandoah Valley, with orders to block the advance of General Jubal Early's Confederates and seal off the rebel breadbasket once and for all. In September 1864 Sheridan defeated Early at Winchester and Fisher's Hill, securing a brigadier's star in the regular army as a reward.

Sheridan's greatest triumph, however, came as the result of a Union defeat. While Sheridan was absent at a meeting, his army was taken by surprise at Cedar Creek on October 19, 1864. Sheridan, twenty miles away in Winchester, heard the roar of battle and galloped to the sound of the guns. His appearance electrified his stricken army; they rallied and crushed Early's Confederates. "Sheridan's ride," as it was called, became one of the most memorable episodes of the Civil War, soon celebrated in poem, story, and painting.

With the rebel army destroyed, Sheridan and his "robbers," as his army was thereafter known, ravaged the Shenandoah Valley so that it could never again support an invading army from the South. Sheridan boasted that a crow would be compelled to carry his own rations when crossing the valley.

President Abraham Lincoln, his reelection hopes given a timely boost by the victory at Cedar Creek, appointed Sheridan a major general in the regular army. Although only thirty-four, Sheridan now stood with Grant and Sherman in the front rank of Union heroes.

Marching southward, Sheridan rejoined Grant in time for the last attack on General Robert E. Lee's Army of Northern Virginia. At Appomattox it was Sheridan's troops who blocked Lee's final line of retreat and compelled his surrender.[5]

Immediately after Appomattox Sheridan was ordered to Texas where he provided moral and material support to the forces of Benito Juárez in their struggle with Maximilian, the puppet of the French emperor Louis Napoleon. Sheridan relished the opportunity

---

[5] For Sheridan's Civil War career see Richard O'Connor, *Sheridan the Inevitable* (Indianapolis: Bobbs-Merrill Company, 1953); Joseph Hergesheimer, *Sheridan: A Military Narrative* (Boston: Houghton Mifflin Company, 1931); Edward J. Stackpole, *Sheridan in the Shenandoah: Jubal Early's Nemesis* (Harrisburg, Pa.: Stackpole Company, 1961); Lawrence A. Frost, *The Phil Sheridan Album: A Pictorial Biography of Philip Henry Sheridan* (Seattle: Superior Publishing Company, 1968); and Philip Henry Sheridan, *Personal Memoirs of P. H. Sheridan. General United States Army*, 2 vols. (New York: Charles L. Webster & Company, 1888).

2. Major General Philip H. Sheridan, 1864.

to confront French troops in battle. No battles were necessary, however, for Juárez's troops, supplied by Sheridan, defeated the imperialists.

Sheridan was also in charge of the defeated rebel states of Texas and Louisiana, and in this task he was not as successful. His enthusiastic application of the relatively harsh Reconstruction policies of the congressional Radical Republicans led President Andrew Johnson to dismiss him from his command on July 31, 1867.

Reassigned to command the Department of the Missouri, which included present Kansas, Oklahoma (Indian Territory), New Mexico, and Colorado, Sheridan found the task of Indian fighting far more congenial work. In 1868 he directed a masterful winter campaign against the Cheyenne Indians and allied tribes. In sharp encounters at the Washita River in November 1868, at Soldier Springs the following month, and at Summit Springs in July 1869, Sheridan's troopers broke the power of the Cheyennes and compelled them to settle on an Indian Territory reservation. The campaign won Sheridan an enviable reputation as an Indian fighter.

When Grant was inaugurated as president in March 1869, he appointed Sheridan lieutenant general and gave him command of the Division of the Missouri. This vast command extended from Chicago on the east to the western borders of Montana, Wyoming, Utah, and New Mexico on the west, and from the Canadian line on the north to the Rio Grande on the south.

Within the boundaries of Sheridan's division lived most of the Indian population of the United States: Sioux, Northern and Southern Cheyennes, Kiowas, Comanches, Arapahos, Utes, Kickapoos, and Apaches all battled Sheridan's troopers. Before he left his frontier post to assume the position of commanding general of the army in 1883, Sheridan planned and directed the greatest Indian campaigns of the century.[6]

Sheridan's pragmatism and elastic ethics made him the perfect frontier soldier for an expansionist republic. He ruthlessly carried out the dictates of his government, never faltering in his conviction that what he did was right. He viewed all Indians as members of an inferior race embracing a primitive culture. He felt them to be inordinately barbarous in war, which he attributed to a natural, ingrained savageness of the race. They formed, in Sheridan's mind, a stone-age barrier to the inevitable advance of white, Christian civilization. Sheridan not only favored this advance but also proudly saw himself as its instrument.

[6] For Sheridan's western career see Paul Andrew Hutton, *Phil Sheridan and His Army* (Lincoln: University of Nebraska Press, 1985).

3. Major General Philip H. Sheridan, 1868.

Although he denied uttering it, the infamous quote that "the only good Indian is a dead Indian" became synonymous with Sheridan and his Indian policy. The sentiment did not originate with the general; nevertheless, the statement has the ring of typical Sheridan rhetoric. He certainly dedicated much of his career to making the cruel sentiment come true.[7]

The torch, to Sheridan, was as powerful a weapon as the sword. In order to break the power of the plains tribes Sheridan proposed to undermine their economy and impoverish them, as well as kill their warriors in battle. This was exactly what he had done in the Shenandoah Valley in 1864.

"I do not hold war to mean simply that lines of men shall engage each other in battle," Sheridan declared, ". . . this is but a duel, in which one combatant seeks the other's life; war means much more, and is far worse than this." Sheridan was convinced that success in war depended upon the destruction of the enemy homeland so as to undermine the will to resist. Destruction of property would bring about a quick surrender, according to Sheridan, because "reduction to poverty brings prayers for peace more surely and more quickly than does the destruction of human life."[8]

In order to apply his philosophy of total war to the Indians, Sheridan believed it to be essential to destroy the great buffalo herds. The buffalo not only provided a rich commissary for the plains tribes but also gave the Indians an excuse to continue their traditional nomadic movements. This led them off their reservations and into collision with whites. Several treaties, such as the 1868 Fort Laramie Treaty with the Sioux, gave the Indians the legal right to hunt in certain areas off the reservation so long as the buffalo ranged in sufficient numbers to justify the chase. Sheridan hoped to quickly reduce the buffalo population and thus terminate this hunting right.

The general applauded the activities of the white hunters who began slaughtering the buffalo in the early 1870s for their hides. In 1867 the number of buffalo was conservatively estimated at fifteen million, but by the mid-1880s the hide hunters had reduced the great herds to a pitiful remnant numbering in the hundreds.[9]

---

[7] Sheridan's Indian policy is discussed in Paul A. Hutton, "Phil Sheridan's Pyrrhic Victory: The Piegan Massacre, Army Politics, and the Transfer Debate," *Montana the Magazine of Western History*, 32 (Spring 1982): 32-43; and Joseph G. Dawson III, "The Alpha-Omega Man: General Phil Sheridan," *Red River Valley Historical Review*, III (Spring 1978): 147-63.

[8] Sheridan, *Personal Memoirs*, 1: 487-88.

[9] For the activities of the hide hunters see Wayne Gard, *The Great Buffalo Hunt*

4. *Buffalo Hunt #7*, by Charles M. Russell, depicts the Indian method of buffalo hunting before the advent of the white hide hunters. Unlike the hide hunters, Cody hunted in the manner of the Indians.

John R. Cook, himself a hide hunter on the southern plains in the 1870s, reported an 1875 message from Sheridan to the Texas state legislature in which the general urged the extermination of the great herds. The legislature was considering a bill to protect the buffalo in Texas, which Sheridan protested. Instead of outlawing the slaughter, declared Sheridan, the legislature should strike a bronze medal, with a dead buffalo on one side and a discouraged Indian on the other, and bestow it on the hunters. "These men have done in the last two years, and will do more in the next years, to settle the vexed Indian question, than the entire regular army has done in the last thirty years," the general declared. "They are destroying the Indians' commissary; and it is a well known fact that an army losing its base of supplies is placed at a great disadvantage. Send them powder and lead, if you will; but for the sake of a lasting peace, let them kill, skin, and sell until the buffaloes are exterminated."[10]

The extermination of these animals appeared, at least at first, to be an impossible task because of their immense numbers. During his 1868 southern plains Indian campaign, Sheridan was astounded by the size of the buffalo herds. According to the general's aide, Lieutenant Colonel John Schuyler Crosby, Sheridan halted the column late one afternoon while marching between the Cimarron and South Canadian Rivers in Indian Territory and asked the assembled officers to estimate the number of buffalo they had seen that day. The soldiers had been passing through the buffalo country since dawn. The animals had covered the countryside, quietly grazing, in immense detached herds numbering from five thousand to twenty thousand each. Each of the ten officers, including experienced frontier fighters George Custer and George Forsyth, put down his estimate on a piece of paper, and they then compared notes. The average of all the estimates was 243,000.

During the same campaign, Sheridan and his quartermaster, Major Henry Inman, attempted to calculate the number of buffalo that ranged between Camp Supply, Indian Territory, and Fort Dodge, Kansas. They had observed an enormous herd, migrating northward, that had extended over one hundred miles in width and was of undetermined length. They at first estimated over one

(New York: Alfred A. Knopf, 1959); Mari Sandoz, *The Buffalo Hunters: The Story of the Hide Men* (New York: Hastings House, 1954); and E. Douglas Branch, *The Hunting of the Buffalo* (New York: D. Appleton and Company, 1929).

[10] John R. Cook, *The Border and the Buffalo: An Untold Story of the Southwest Plains* (New York: Citadel Press, 1967), 163-64.

5. Buffalo trails cross the Saline River Valley near Bunker Hill, Kansas. This country, similar in terrain to that crossed by Sheridan's 1871 hunting party, is just east of Fort Hays.

billion animals but revised that downward to over one hundred million. They believed that number to be a conservative one but hesitated to make it public for fear that no one would believe them.[11]

After the destruction of the southern herd in the early 1870s, Sheridan worked to insure the same fate for the northern herd.

[11] Martin S. Garretson, *The American Bison: The Story of Its Extermination as a Wild Species and Its Restoration under Federal Protection* (New York: New York Zoological Society, 1938), 63-64.

The buffalos were divided into northern and southern herds by first the overland

When, in 1881, the government considered protecting what was left of the herds, Sheridan vigorously opposed such action. "If I could learn that every buffalo in the northern herd were killed I would be glad," the general wrote the War Department. "The destruction of this herd would do more to keep Indians quiet than anything else that could happen. Since the destruction of the southern herd, which formerly roamed from Texas to the Platte, the Indians in that section have given us no trouble."[12]

Sheridan's sponsorship of several civilian hunting parties onto the plains thus secured the dual benefits of furthering his policy of exterminating the buffalo while at the same time currying the favor of powerful, influential citizens. An avid sportsman, Sheridan liked to combine business with pleasure on these western jaunts. Usually, however, the press of military business kept him from joining the hunts, and so he provided his friends with letters of introduction. These letters enabled them to obtain supplies, equipment, military escorts, knowledgeable scouts, and other types of assistance at frontier military posts.[13]

These requests for escorts and supplies often taxed the meagre

---

wagon roads and then the transcontinental railroads. It was the southern herd that Sheridan's hunting party sought in 1871. The most extensive years of hunting on the southern plains were from 1870 to 1874 and on the northern plains from 1876 to 1883. The best estimates of buffalo population are in Frank Gilbert Roe, *The North American Buffalo: A Critical Study of the Species in Its Wild State* (Toronto: University of Toronto Press, 1951), 416-66. Also see Tom McHugh, *The Time of the Buffalo* (New York: Alfred A. Knopf, 1972); Francis Haines, *The Buffalo* (New York: Thomas Y. Crowell Company, 1970); David A. Dary, *The Buffalo Book: The Full Saga of the American Animal* (Chicago: Swallow Press, 1974); and J. Albert Rorabacher, *The American Buffalo in Transition: A Historical and Economic Survey of the Bison in America* (Saint Cloud, Minn.: North Star Books, 1970).

[12] Sheridan to the Adjutant General, October 13, 1881, Box 29, Philip H. Sheridan Papers, Library of Congress. Ironically, in 1883 Sheridan began to work to expand the boundaries of Yellowstone National Park so as to provide a better refuge for western game animals, including the buffalo. Two of his companions on the 1871 buffalo hunt, John Schuyler Crosby, appointed territorial governor of Montana in 1882, and Buffalo Bill Cody, aided the general in this crusade. Before his death from a heart attack on August 5, 1888, Sheridan succeeded in blocking the schemes of capitalists to gain monopoly rights to the park, secured competent military protection for the park's wildlife, and initiated a broad-based crusade for the expansion of the park's boundaries. See Paul A. Hutton, "Phil Sheridan's Crusade for Yellowstone," *American History Illustrated*, XIX (February 1985): 10-15.

[13] For examples of Sheridan's help in providing military escorts and other types of assistance to friends visiting the frontier, see Sheridan to William T. Sherman, May 1, 1874, July 31, 1879, Box 39, Sheridan Papers; Sheridan to Luther P. Bradley, Nov. 30, 1881, Box 30, ibid.; Sheridan to James Brisbin, May 10, 1879, Box 23, ibid.; Sheridan to Alfred Terry, May 10, 1879, Box 23, ibid.; Sheridan to Frank Thomson, May 10, 1879, Box 23, ibid.; Sheridan to George Crook, April 2, 1880, Box 26, ibid.;

6. R. M. Wright sits atop a pile of thousands of buffalo hides in Rath and Wright's Buffalo Hide Yard, Dodge City, Kansas, in 1874. In the background workers operate a press to bale the hides for shipment east.

resources of frontier forts. So burdensome did the requests become to the commander of Fort Custer, Montana, Lieutenant Colonel Andrew J. Alexander, that he protested the letters to his superiors. Alexander's post was near Yellowstone National Park, so he found

Sheridan to Commanding Officer, Fort Ellis, Montana, May 8, 1880, Box 26, ibid.; and Sheridan to Ranald S. Mackenzie, Nov. 11, 1882, Box 33, ibid.

For three other Sheridan hunting trips in the West, see William E. Strong, *Canadian River Hunt* (Norman: University of Oklahoma Press, 1960); *Journey through the Yellowstone National Park and Northwestern Wyoming, 1883: Photographs of Party and Scenery along the Route Traveled, and Copies of the Associated Press Dispatches sent Whilst En Route* (n.p. 1883); and Sheridan, *Personal Memoirs*, 2: 351-54.

7. Buffalo hides loaded on bull-train wagons, Dodge City, Kansas, 1874.

himself a particular target of such letters. The provision of transportation, supplies, and escorts to various parties of sportsmen and tourists with letters from Sheridan drained the resources of Alexander's isolated post.[14]

Sheridan, always a bit sensitive about providing military assistance to friends, businessmen, and other prominent tourists traveling west, checked with Secretary of War William W. Belknap in 1872 on the propriety of such action. "I have no objection to such reasonable facilities being granted as may be done," Belknap replied, "when such action is consistent with the interests of the service."[15] Since Belknap resigned his office in 1876 after being caught accepting kickbacks from army contractors, he hardly represented an unimpeachable source.

Despite the fact that he had this official sanction for letters of introduction, Sheridan nevertheless apologized to Alexander for placing an undue burden on the resources of Fort Custer. He promised to write no more letters for tourists visiting that post. He was not nearly as gracious, however, in a communication to General William T. Sherman, in which he denied providing any letters to tourists visiting Fort Custer. Alexander, it seems, had made a serious career mistake. "It is a careless statement for a man of his rank to make," Sheridan grumbled. A day of reckoning would obviously come.[16]

The buffalo hunt described by Davies in this book was the largest of the private hunts sponsored by Sheridan on the plains. Even it, however, paled in comparison to the expedition Sheridan staged the following year for the Grand Duke Alexis of Russia. The 1871 hunt was, in many ways, a practice run for the more important royal hunting party that Sheridan escorted west in 1872.

The Grand Duke Alexis, twenty-one-year-old third son of the Russian Czar, wanted a taste of western soldiering and hunting during his 1871–1872 visit to the United States. A tour of eastern cities kept the Grand Duke busy until January 1872, which gave Sheridan time to oversee martial law and relief efforts in fire-devastated Chicago in the months between his two great buffalo hunts.

The hunt was on a truly spectacular scale. Two companies of infantry, two companies of cavalry, and the regimental band of the

[14] Sheridan endorsement, Sept. 15, 1881, Box 29, Sheridan Papers; Sheridan to Sherman, Nov. 16, 1881, Box 30, ibid.

[15] William W. Belknap to Sheridan, May 14, 1872, Box 7, Sheridan Papers; Sheridan to Belknap, May 11, 1872, Box 7, ibid.

[16] Sheridan to Sherman, Nov. 16, 1881, Box 30, Sheridan Papers.

Second Cavalry made up the military escort. Lieutenant Colonel George A. Custer, then on Reconstruction duty in Kentucky, and Lieutenant Colonel George A. Forsyth, Sheridan's military secretary and the hero of the 1868 stand at Beecher's Island, were along to allow the royal guest to hobnob with authentic Indian fighters. Lieutenant Edward M. Hayes, regimental quartermaster for the Fifth Cavalry who had been in charge of supply for the 1871 hunt, was appointed quartermaster for the 1872 hunt as well.

Sheridan selected Buffalo Bill Cody as guide. The general ordered Cody to remain at Fort McPherson, even though the Fifth Cavalry had been transferred to Arizona, in order to use him on the royal hunt. Cody's first assignment was to convince Chief Spotted Tail to bring one hundred Brulé Sioux south to entertain the Grand Duke and join in the hunt.

When Sheridan and his royal guest reached the main hunting camp on Red Willow Creek, Nebraska, some sixty miles south of Fort McPherson, on January 13, 1872, they found everything in readiness. The hunt proved a success with dozens of dead buffalo soon littering the plains. There were Indian dances, war stories from Custer and Forsyth, and tall tales by Cody to keep Alexis's evenings as lively as his days.

After two days of hunting, the party decamped for the railroad, which was to take them to Denver. The Grand Duke toured Denver and nearby mining camps before setting off after another large buffalo herd located near Kit Carson, Colorado. This hunt was even more successful than the one in Nebraska. Alexis, well satisfied with his western adventure, then returned east by special train to St. Louis. Sheridan departed for Chicago, putting Alexis under Custer's care for additional tours of Louisville and New Orleans. The hunt also proved a resounding diplomatic success; Sheridan even received a decoration from the Russian Czar in recognition of his services to the royal family.[17]

[17] For an overview of the Grand Duke's visit see William F. Zornow, "When the Czar and Grant Were Friends," *Mid-America*, XLIII (July 1961): 164-81. For a contemporary account, compiled from newspaper clippings, see *The Grand Duke Alexis in the United States of America* (New York: Interland Publishing, 1972). For details of the hunt see Don Russell, *The Lives and Legends of Buffalo Bill* (Norman: University of Oklahoma Press, 1960), 174-84; William F. Cody, *The Life of Hon. William F. Cody Known as Buffalo Bill* (Lincoln: University of Nebraska Press, 1978), 295-305; Marshall Sprague, *A Gallery of Dudes* (Lincoln: University of Nebraska Press, 1979), 95-117; James Albert Hadley, "A Royal Buffalo Hunt," *Transactions of the Kansas State Historical Society*, X (1907–1908): 564-80; John I. White, "Red Carpet for a Romanoff," *American West*, IX (January 1972): 5-9; and Buffalo Bill [William F. Cody], "Famous Hunting Parties of the Plains," *Cosmopolitan*, XVII (June 1894): 131-43.

8. *Great Royal Buffalo Hunt*, by Louis Maurer, depicts Chief Spotted Tail, Buffalo Bill Cody, and General Phil Sheridan during the Grand Duke Alexis's 1872 hunt. Born in Germany in 1832, Maurer studied mathematical drawing as a young man, attending school in Mainz. His family came to the United States in 1851, and he took a job as a staff artist for Currier and Ives. In 1885 Maurer made his first extensive trip to the West as the guest of Cody. That trip served as the inspiration for this painting, completed in 1894. Although colorful and full of action, the painting is not accurate. Maurer depicts Cody as he looked in the 1880s and has armed him with a Winchester, model 1873, for the 1872 hunt.

Buffalo Bill left the party at North Platte, Nebraska, much to the regret of Alexis, who was quite taken with the young plainsman. The Grand Duke presented Cody with several valuable gifts, including jeweled cuff links and studs. But the Grand Duke's gifts paled in comparison to the value of some timely advice from Sheridan. At the conclusion of the September hunt James Gordon Bennett, Jr., had invited Cody to be his guest in New York, and Sheridan now urged the scout to take advantage of that opportunity. The general secured Cody a leave of absence with pay from his military scouting duties. Anson Stager provided railroad passes for the trip east, and Bennett quickly sent out five hundred dollars to cover expenses.[18]

Cody worked up his courage and headed east in February 1872, first stopping in Chicago to visit General Sheridan. He stayed with the general and his brother, Michael V. Sheridan, in their attractive, two-story bachelor home at 708 South Michigan Avenue. Before foraying out into society Cody was taken to Marshall Field's by Mike Sheridan and decked out in appropriate evening wear.

Buffalo Bill, noticing no one else on the streets of Chicago with shoulder-length hair, decided to get a haircut, but Mike Sheridan vetoed the plan. He suggested instead that a formal top hat might be in order to keep the flowing locks in place. But tall evening headgear did not suit Cody, who instead took to sporting a western Stetson to top off his new white tie and tails and patent leather shoes. In this striking costume he sallied forth with the Sheridan brothers to sample Chicago society, often in company with Sam Johnson, Anson Stager, and Charles Wilson, all alumni of the September hunt.[19]

These scouting expeditions into high society proved challenging to the shy plainsman. A dinner in the fashionable Chicago suburb of Riverside almost proved too much. "On this occasion," Cody later recalled, "I became so embarrassed that it was more difficult for me to face the throng of beautiful ladies than it would have been to confront a hundred hostile Indians. This was my first trip to the East, and I had not yet become accustomed to being stared at."[20] Sheridan, who delighted in a good joke, undoubtedly relished his young friend's discomfort.

After a few days in Chicago, Cody boarded a train for New York City, stopping en route to see Niagara Falls and play the gawking

[18] Cody, *Life of Hon. William F. Cody*, 305-7; Russell, *Buffalo Bill*, 180.

[19] Elizabeth Jane Leonard and Julia Cody Goodman, *Buffalo Bill: King of the Old West* (New York: Library Publishers, 1955), 210-11.

[20] Cody, *Life of Hon. William F. Cody*, 307.

tourist in Rochester, New York. Upon reaching New York City he was met by John G. Heckscher, appointed as "a committee of one" by the other alumni of the buffalo hunt to escort their guest to the Union Club. A welcoming dinner, hosted by James Gordon Bennett, Jr., and Leonard W. Jerome, awaited Cody at the Union Club. It was a grand affair, and the new "lion of the West" was an immediate success with New York's "better class" of men.

Buffalo Bill, however, was anxious to find an old acquaintance who most assuredly did not number among the city's upper crust. With Heckscher scouting the paved trail for him, Cody sought out Ned Buntline at the Brevoort Place Hotel.[21]

Buntline, whose real name was Edward Zane Carroll Judson, was a stumpy, plump little man with a zest for life and a talent for writing wonderful trash. He was a master of the dime novel, claiming to have written half a dozen of them in one week. He went through several fortunes and six wives, some of whom he was married to simultaneously.

Born in the state of New York on March 20, 1823, Buntline went to sea as a youth, eventually becoming a midshipman in the United States Navy. He found himself in the Florida naval force of Lieutenant John T. McLaughlin, called the Mosquito Squadron, and participated in the Seminole Indian War. Naval life proved too tame for Ned, even with an Indian war on, so he resigned from the service. The navy did, however, gave him his famous pseudonym— a *buntline* is the naval word for a rope at the bottom of a square sail.

Writing and women were Ned's great passions, and he pursued both with a vengeance. He was widely published, even writing for journals as good as *Knickerbocker*. For a time he served as editor of the struggling *Western Literary Journal*. This promising editorial career nearly came to a premature close at the end of a rope in 1846. In Nashville the twenty-two-year-old literary lion had a brief dalliance with a young lady who was unfortunately burdened with a jealous husband. As was the custom in Tennessee in those days, a duel followed the inevitable exposure of the affair. Ned was an excellent shot, a good talent for an editor, and promptly shot the husband between the eyes. Being a law-abiding man, Buntline turned himself in to the local authorities. Before long a mob stormed the jail and carried Buntline off to the public square and hanged him. Fortunately for Ned they were an impatient bunch, leaving their victim to dangle while they headed for the nearest saloon to celebrate. Ned's friends cut him down and whisked him

[21] Ibid., 308.

away. He headed for the safer climes of Philadelphia, a bruised but wiser man—wiser at least about mobs if not about women.

In New York City in 1848 he established a paper, *Ned Buntline's Own,* which he envisioned as a nativist competitor to James Gordon Bennett's *New York Herald.* Buntline's paper published fictional pieces by its owner, as well as diatribes against liquor, gambling, and prostitution. Ned knew all about these vices from firsthand experience. The paper also championed the anti-immigrant Know Nothing Party, and Buntline was jailed in St. Louis in 1852 for instigating an anti-German riot.

During the Civil War Ned served in a New York volunteer regiment for two years, briefly attaining the rank of sergeant. He later claimed to have been a chief-of-scouts with the rank of colonel.[22]

After the war Buntline continued his writing, supplementing his income with temperance lectures. On July 24, 1869, he was scheduled to rail against the evils of strong drink at Fort McPherson. Before the lecture, however, he learned that Major William H. Brown was to lead a detachment of the Fifth Cavalry out after an Indian raiding party. Always in search of a good story, Buntline volunteered to accompany the troops.

Major Brown introduced the celebrated writer to the Fifth Cavalry's chief-of-scouts. Cody was impressed, feeling that the writer had the look of a soldier about him.

"Colonel Judson, I am glad to meet you," Buffalo Bill declared. "The Major tells me that you are to accompany us on the scout."

"Yes, my boy, so I am," Ned replied. "I was to deliver a temperance lecture tonight, but no lectures for me when there is a prospect for a fight."[23]

They found no Indians along the North Platte, but Buntline discovered Cody to be a treasure trove of frontier lore. Cody took a liking to his new acquaintance, loaning him his own horse. When the scouting party concluded at Fort Sedgwick, Buntline headed east, promising to keep in touch.

On December 23, 1869, the *New York Weekly* carried the first installment of Buntline's "Buffalo Bill, the King of Border Men." The author claimed every word of his tale to be true, even though it had absolutely nothing to do with Cody. The story was a fictional reworking of the already well-publicized Civil War exploits of

[22] For Ned Buntline's fabulous career see Jay Monaghan, *The Great Rascal: The Life and Adventures of Ned Buntline* (Boston: Little, Brown and Co., 1952). For the history of dime novels see Daryl Jones, *The Dime Novel Western* (Bowling Green, Ohio: Popular Press, 1978).

[23] Cody, *Life of Hon. William F. Cody,* 263.

9. Buffalo Bill Cody in 1871, as he looked at the time of Sheridan's buffalo hunt.

Cody's close friend, James Butler "Wild Bill" Hickok. Nevertheless, from Buntline's story was born the legend of Buffalo Bill.

Back at Fort McPherson the real Buffalo Bill was highly flattered by the tale even if none of it was true. When his son was born on November 26, 1870, he proposed to name him after Colonel Judson. Cooler heads fortunately prevailed, and the lad was instead named Kit Carson Cody.[24]

Cody, most anxious to see his literary benefactor again, enjoyed a warm reunion with Buntline at the Brevoort Place. Ned, quickly developing a proprietary attitude toward Buffalo Bill, insisted that his young friend remain at the hotel as his guest. Cody, not wanting to offend Bennett, finally agreed to divide his time between the Union Club and the Brevoort Place. Cody was overwhelmed by invitations, with formal dinners in his honor given by Bennett and the banker August Belmont. On one occasion Cody got lost on a scout through New York's stone canyons and missed a dinner in his honor staged by Bennett. To atone for this carelessness he accompanied the newspaperman to the Liederkranz masked ball. Cody, of course, went dressed in full buckskin costume. The other guests at the Academy of Music gawked at this western rustic, delighted that the authentic Buffalo Bill had, as the *New York Herald* announced, "come from the land of the buffalo and red skin to see for himself the difference between an Indian powwow and a genuine masquerade."[25]

The high point of Cody's visit came on February 20, 1872, when he went to the Bowery Theater, as Buntline's guest, for the opening night of *Buffalo Bill, the King of Border Men*. Buntline's *New York Weekly* stories had been dramatized by Fred G. Maeder in 1871 into a little play full of blood-and-thunder action. J. B. Studley made a stalwart Buffalo Bill, but when the audience learned that the original item was sitting in Buntline's box they thunderously demanded his appearance on the stage. Timid and embarrassed, Cody went before the footlights for the first time in his life, bowed, and mumbled a few inaudible words of thanks to the crowd.

The theater owner, deeply impressed by this reception, if not by the scout's stage ability, promptly offered Cody five hundred dollars a week to replace Studley as Buffalo Bill. Feeling that a government mule would make a better candidate for the role, Bill declined the offer. "I didn't have the requisite cheek to undertake a thing of that sort," Cody declared.[26]

Even without the real Buffalo Bill the play had a successful

[24] Russell, *Buffalo Bill*, 159-60.
[25] Monaghan, *Great Rascal*, 15.
[26] Ibid., 15; Cody, *Life of Hon. William F. Cody*, 311; Russell, *Buffalo Bill*, 181-82.

eight-week run at the Bowery Theater before touring in other major cities. It was greeted by enthusiastic audiences, if not good notices, wherever it played.

General Sheridan visited the city a few days later and was naturally anxious to see how his friend was faring. Bill, warming to public acclaim, informed the general that he had "struck the best camp" he had ever seen, and he requested an extension of his leave. Sheridan gladly granted this boon but warned his favorite scout that the Third Cavalry, soon to reach its new station at Fort McPherson, would need his services.[27]

After visiting relatives in West Chester, Pennsylvania, near Philadelphia, in company with Buntline, Cody finally brought his eastern sojourn to an end and headed back to Fort McPherson. Along the way he got roaring drunk, which was not unusual for him, and lost his trunk, so that he reported to his new commanding officer, Colonel Joseph J. Reynolds, Third Cavalry, wearing a formal evening suit and a tall stovepipe hat. It was somehow fitting, for the East had taken ahold of Buffalo Bill and he would never again be the same.

Fighting Indians seemed tame to Cody after the heady excitement of his New York trip. Nevertheless, his baptism in high society did not dull his skills as a scout. On April 26, 1872, near the south fork of Nebraska's Loup River, Cody led a squad of soldiers in a running battle with Indian raiders, which won him the Medal of Honor on May 22, 1872.[28]

Captain Charles Meinhold, in the letter of commendation describing the sharp engagement with the Indians, noted that "Mr. William Cody's reputation for bravery and skill as a guide is so well established that I need not say anything else but that he acted in his usual manner."[29] Meinhold's words are typical of the high regard in which experienced frontier soldiers held Cody. Phil Sheridan, William Emory, Eugene Carr, Wesley Merritt, Charles King, Anson Mills, and other army officers praised Cody lavishly both before and after he became nationally famous. Cody's exploits, although later exaggerated by press agents and show business hype, were authentic. Later writers who attempted to downplay his scouting activities or who treated him as just one of many comparable army guides either purposefully ignored the evidence or were unaware of the facts.

Cody ranks with Ben Clark, Frank Grouard, Charles Reynolds,

[27] Cody, *Life of Hon. William F. Cody*, 312.
[28] Russell, *Buffalo Bill*, 186-87. By act of Congress on June 16, 1916, Cody's medal was taken away since, as a civilian, he was not eligible for a military award.
[29] Ibid., 187.

and Frank North as one of the few truly outstanding army scouts in the post–Civil War Indian conflicts. In one twelve-month period, for example, from October 1868 to October 1869, Cody, as chief-of-scouts for the Fifth Cavalry, participated in seven expeditions against the Indians, engaging in nine fights with the hostiles.[30] Few soldiers experienced that much action in a decade of frontier service. All of Cody's frontier exploits, including sixteen Indian battles, occurred before his thirty-second birthday, for after 1876 he devoted his time exclusively to show business.

Cody was a true child of the frontier. Born in Scott County, Iowa, on February 26, 1846, William Frederick was the third child born to Isaac and Mary Laycock Cody. Isaac Cody moved his family to the newly organized Kansas Territory in 1854, settling near Fort Leavenworth, where he became a prominent advocate of the Free-Soil cause. While speaking against the extension of slavery into Kansas on September 18, 1854, Isaac was pulled from his platform and stabbed by several proslavery men. Although he recovered well enough to prosper economically and to win election to the Free-Soil Topeka legislature in 1856, Isaac was continually plagued by the wound, finally dying on March 10, 1857. To Bill Cody, his father was a martyr, having "shed the first blood in the cause of the freedom of Kansas."[31]

With the family in financial straits after his father's death, young Cody went to work for the freighting company of Alexander Majors and William Russell. The company soon after contracted with the government to haul supplies for Colonel Albert Sidney Johnston's army, which was then marching west to convince Brigham Young and his followers of the necessity of obeying the federal officials set over them in the so-called Utah or Mormon War of 1857. On this trip Cody struck up a friendship with another company employee, James Butler "Wild Bill" Hickok. Wild Bill, nine years senior to Cody, appointed himself as the eleven-year-old boy's guardian on the trip. They remained warm friends until Hickok's death in 1876.[32]

When Russell, Majors, and Waddell initiated the short-lived but glamorous Pony Express in 1860, Cody served as a rider. He is

[30] Ibid., 160.

[31] Cody, *Life of Hon. William F. Cody*, 43. For Cody's early life see ibid., 17-63; Russell, *Buffalo Bill*, 3-26; Leonard and Goodman, *Buffalo Bill*, 25-72.

[32] Joseph G. Rosa, *They Called Him Wild Bill: The Life and Adventures of James Butler Hickok* (Norman: University of Oklahoma Press, 1974), 22-23; Russell, *Buffalo Bill*, 33-34.

credited with the third longest Pony Express ride: 322 miles in twenty-one hours and forty minutes, using twenty-one horses.[33]

With the outbreak of the Civil War, Cody quit the Pony Express and joined a band of Kansas Jayhawkers preying upon neighboring Missourians. Cody, anxious to avenge his father's murder and the depredations of Missouri "Border Ruffians" against his family and friends, felt no pangs of conscience about his horse-stealing forays into Missouri. Mary Cody, however, recognized that thievery was still thievery even if hidden behind a flag, and she persuaded her fifteen-year-old son to quit the Jayhawkers. Bill joined instead a band of irregular militia, called Red Legs, commanded by William S. Tough. They were only slightly more respectable than the Jayhawkers. This home guard battled rebel guerillas led by the infamous William C. Quantrill.

Cody readily admitted that these were not his best days. "I entered upon a dissolute and reckless life—to my shame be it said— and associated with gamblers, drunkards, and bad characters generally." After one particularly rowdy night in February 1864, Cody enlisted as a private in the Seventh Kansas Volunteer Cavalry. He claimed to have passed out under "the influence of bad whiskey" and then awoke to find himself a soldier. "I did not remember how or when I had enlisted," he mused, "but I saw I was in for it, and that it would not do for me to endeavor to back out."[34] Private Cody served in the regiment until the end of the war, participating in several battles as well as acting as scout and dispatch rider.[35]

With the war over Cody took himself a bride, Louisa Frederici of St. Louis, and attempted to settle down to the respectable life of a hotelkeeper at his Salt Creek Valley home. It was not to be, for he was devoid of business skills, and within a year he headed west to seek employment with the army. Hickok was scouting out of Fort Ellsworth, Kansas, at the time, and he got his friend a job as guide at the post. While at Fort Ellsworth Cody became acquainted with Lieutenant Colonel George A. Custer, Seventh Cavalry, then just commencing his frontier career.

Custer asked Cody to scout for the Seventh Cavalry in a proposed summer campaign against the Cheyennes, but an offer to hunt buffalo to feed workers on the Kansas Pacific Railroad proved more attractive. The firm of Goddard Brothers had the contract to board the railway workers, and they employed Cody to provide twelve

---

[33] Russell, *Buffalo Bill*, 49-50.
[34] Cody, *Life of Hon. William F. Cody*, 135.
[35] For Cody's Civil War career see ibid., 134-40; Russell, *Buffalo Bill*, 55-72.

buffalo a day to feed the men. He was to be paid five hundred dollars a month for this dangerous work, a princely sum in 1867.[36]

In eight months' time, from October 1867 until May 1868, Cody killed 4,280 buffalo for the Kansas Pacific. Mounted on his fleet horse Brigham (named after the Mormon patriarch because he had been purchased from a Utah Indian) and armed with a breechloading .50-caliber Springfield rifle dubbed Lucretia Borgia, Cody became a familiar and welcome sight in the tough, end-of-track railway camps. The workers conferred on him the sobriquet of Buffalo Bill, and it stuck. They even composed a ditty that they sang while working on the construction gangs.

> Buffalo Bill, Buffalo Bill
> Never missed and never will;
> Always aims and shoots to kill
> And the company pays his buffalo bill.[37]

A combination of bad weather and hostile Indians temporarily halted construction of the Kansas Pacific when end-of-track reached Sheridan, Kansas. There was thus no reason for Goddard Brothers to renew Cody's contract when it ended in May 1868. Cody was not unemployed for long. With a new war brewing with the Cheyenne Indians and their allies, the army promptly hired him. Cody went to work at Fort Larned for Colonel William B. Hazen, the Indian superintendent for the southern plains, whose job it was to protect friendly Indians while identifying potential hostiles.[38]

It was while working for Hazen that Cody first came to the attention of General Sheridan. Cody was sent from Fort Larned to Fort Hays, a distance of sixty-five miles, to report to General Sheridan that some of the Kiowas and Comanches had joined the hostiles. This disturbing news forced Sheridan to change his troop dispositions. It was now vital that he get new orders through to Fort Dodge, but he could not find a scout willing to undertake the ride. "This too being a particularly dangerous route—several couriers having been killed on it—it was impossible to get one of the various 'Petes,' 'Jacks,' or 'Jims' hanging around Hays City to take my communication," Sheridan later recalled. "Cody learning of the strait I

[36] Russell, *Buffalo Bill*, 88-90.

[37] Ibid., 90. Cody sold Brigham in 1868 because he did not want to take a chance of killing the horse in scouting for the army. For Cody's horses see Agnes Wright Spring, *Buffalo Bill and His Horses* (Denver: Bradford-Robinson, 1968).

[38] For Colonel Hazen's role on the southern plains see Marvin E. Kroeker, *Great Plains Command: William B. Hazen in the Frontier West* (Norman: University of Oklahoma Press, 1976), 70-90.

10. *Buffalo Hunt*, by Jacob Gogolin, was painted in 1926. Gogolin (1844–1940) was born in Germany and came to the United States in 1902. Gogolin and Cody became good friends after Gogolin moved to Denver, and the artist made several paintings depicting episodes from Cody's life.

was in, manfully came to the rescue, and proposed to make the trip to Dodge, though he had just finished his long and perilous ride from Larned."[39]

Cody carried the dispatches to Fort Dodge, slept for a few hours, and then headed back to Fort Larned with more mail. At Larned, Colonel Hazen immediately recruited him to again make the dangerous ride to Fort Hays with the news that the Kiowas had fled south of the Arkansas River. It was an amazing and heroic ride. Cody covered almost three hundred miles in some fifty-eight hours of riding time, often moving parallel to the hostile Indians he was carrying news about.[40]

Sheridan, profoundly impressed by Cody's "exhibition of endurance and courage," personally appointed him chief-of-scouts for the Fifth Cavalry.[41] Although other scouts were hired only for individual expeditions, Cody continuously served as chief-of-scouts for the Fifth from September 1868 until November 1872, when Ned Buntline finally persuaded him to forsake the frontier for the eastern stage.

Now Ned Buntline was not a man to allow opportunity to slip away. No sooner had he seen Cody off on a westbound train after the New York visit than Ned commenced scribbling a new dime novel. "Buffalo Bill's Best Shot; or, the Heart of Spotted Tail" began its serial run in the *New York Weekly* on March 25, 1872, quickly followed in July by "Buffalo Bill's Last Victory; or, Dove Eye, the Lodge Queen." At the same time Ned barraged Cody with letters promising fame and fortune if he would return east and portray himself on the stage.

Cody recruited another Fort McPherson scout, John B. "Texas Jack" Omohundro, to accompany him to Chicago and join in this novel enterprise. Texas Jack was a Virginian, was the same age as Cody, and had fought in General J.E.B. Stuart's cavalry during the Civil War. After Appomattox he had drifted into Texas, eventually coming north to Kansas on one of the great cattle drives. A chance acquaintance with Wild Bill Hickok got him into the scouting business, and he was soon serving under Cody at Fort McPherson. When General Sheridan sent the Earl of Dunraven, the British politician and war correspondent, to Fort McPherson for a hunt in 1872, it was Texas Jack who guided the distinguished party.[42]

[39] Sheridan, *Personal Memoirs*, 2: 300-301.

[40] Cody, *Life of Hon. William F. Cody*, 187-99; Russell, *Buffalo Bill*, 103.

[41] Sheridan, *Personal Memoirs*, 2: 301.

[42] For the career of Texas Jack Omohundro see Herschel C. Logan, *Buckskin and Satin: The Life of Texas Jack* (Harrisburg, Pa.: Stackpole Company, 1954). Cody was to have guided the Earl of Dunraven's 1872 hunting party, but the arrival of

The Earl of Dunraven had been quite taken by both Buffalo Bill and Texas Jack. Eastern audiences from Chicago to New York soon came to agree with the Earl's glowing description of the scouts.

Both were tall, well-built, active-looking men, with singularly handsome features. . . . Jack, tall and lithe, with light brown close-cropped hair, clear laughing honest blue eyes, and a soft and winning smile, might have sat as a model for a typical modern Anglo-Saxon—if ethnologists will excuse the term. Bill was dark, with quick searching eyes, aquiline nose, and delicately cut features, and he wore his hair falling in long ringlets over his shoulders, in true Western style. As he cantered up, with his flowing locks and broad-brimmed hat, he looked like a picture of a cavalier of olden times.[43]

The scouts-turned-actors were met by Buntline in Chicago on December 12. To their amazement they found that Buntline had no script, even though the play was to open at Nixon's Amphitheatre on December 18. Retreating to his hotel room, Buntline penned *The Scouts of the Prairie* in four hours. An unimpressed *Chicago Tribune* theater critic later asked why it had taken Ned so long to write the play.

Buntline hired ten aspiring thespians off the Chicago streets to portray Indians in his little drama and acquired the services of a lovely Italian actress, Giuseppina Morlacchi, to portray the Indian heroine. Unlike the other members of the cast Morlacchi actually had stage experience; she was well known for introducing the cancan to the United States in 1867.[44]

A crowd estimated at 2,500 crowded into Nixon's Amphitheatre for opening night. The play had no discernible plot, which was fine since Cody forgot all his lines anyway. It did not matter, for the scouts were handsome, Miss Morlacchi fetching as an Italian-accented Indian maiden, and the action nonstop. "The way Jack and I killed Indians was a 'caution,'" Cody recalled. "We would kill them all off in one act, but they would come up again ready for business in the next."[45]

*The Scouts of the Prairie* was a grand success. Even the theater

---

another group of General Sheridan's Chicago friends forced him to turn the chore over entirely to Omohundro. For Dunraven's western hunts see Sprague, *A Gallery of Dudes*, 146-79.

[43] Earl of Dunraven, *Canadian Nights: Being Sketches and Reminiscences of Life and Sport in the Rockies, the Prairies and the Canadian Woods* (New York: Charles Scribner's Sons, 1914), 56.

[44] Monaghan, *Great Rascal*, 19-21; Logan, *Buckskin and Satin*, 101-18.

[45] Cody, *Life of Hon. William F. Cody*, 327.

11. Ned Buntline, Buffalo Bill Cody, Giuseppina Morlacchi, and Texas Jack Omohundro as they appeared during the 1872–1873 theatrical season in "The Scouts of the Prairie."

critics had to admit that it might not be art, but it was certainly entertainment of a unique sort. "On the whole it is not probable that Chicago will ever look upon the like again," declared the *Chicago Tribune*. "Such a combination of incongruous drama, execrable acting, renowned performers, mixed audience, intolerable stench, scalping, blood and thunder, is not likely to be vouchsafed to a city a second time—even Chicago."[46]

[46] Russell, *Buffalo Bill*, 196.

The Western had been born, with Ned Buntline and Buffalo Bill acting as able midwives, and popular, mass-market entertainment was never to be the same again. The play toured St. Louis, Cincinnati, Buffalo, Rochester, Boston, and New York, continually greeted by enthusiastic lowbrow audiences, stunned theater critics, and overflowing box office tills. By the time the tour ended in June 1873, Cody was fully committed to a stage career. He no longer had need of Buntline, and they parted company forever that month.

For the 1873–1874 theatrical season Cody enlisted the pen of Fred G. Maeder, author of the first Buffalo Bill play, to create a new drama for the Buffalo Bill Combination, as his gypsy troupe was now called. *The Scouts of the Plains* opened at Williamsport, Pennsylvania, on September 8. Buffalo Bill and Texas Jack played themselves, of course, with Giuseppina Morlacchi portraying another winsome Indian maiden. In August she and Texas Jack had been married. Co-starring was another authentic western hero, Cody's old friend Wild Bill Hickok. By this time Wild Bill had added to his laurels as scout and Indian fighter by serving as marshal in Hays City and Abilene. Cody figured that the famous gunfighting lawman would be quite a draw.

The life of a thespian did not suit Hickok. For some reason he could never take playacting seriously. One of his favorite amusements was shooting his pistols so close to the legs of the extras playing Indians that instead of dying as they were supposed to, they would jump around the stage, screaming in pain from powder burns. All Cody's efforts to imbue his friend with a proper respect for show business failed, and after one particularly heated exchange Hickok departed in a huff. They met again only once, in Wyoming in July 1876 when Cody was scouting for the Fifth Cavalry and Hickok was heading for the Black Hills boomtown of Deadwood, and for his rendezvous with an assassin's bullet.[47]

The partnership between Cody and Omohundro soon broke up as well, but far more amicably. They concluded that each could make more money on his own, and so they went their separate ways in 1876. Texas Jack and his wife toured successfully in various frontier melodramas until his untimely death in 1880.

For a decade, from 1873 until he left the boards to organize his Wild West show in 1883, Cody toured in various frontier dramas. In every play he starred as Buffalo Bill, with each drama supposedly based on authentic adventures from his own past. It was this connection between history and drama that provided a unique electricity to Cody's stage presence and kept his blood-and-thunder

[47] Rosa, *They Called Him Wild Bill*, 242-61.

12. Wild Bill Hickok, Texas Jack Omohundro, and Buffalo Bill Cody posed for this photograph in Syracuse, New York, near the end of the 1873–1874 theatrical season.

plays popular with the public. People were anxious to see the real Buffalo Bill because he represented a stirring frontier past that was becoming increasingly distant to a rapidly industrializing, urbanized America.

Always conscious of the connection between his stage success and this popular identification of him as an authentic frontiersman, Cody often traveled west during the summers guiding hunting parties—for a handsome fee—and occasionally working for the army as a scout. The line between Buffalo Bill the eastern actor and William F. Cody the frontier scout would become increasingly blurred during these years. Never was this more apparent than during the summer of 1876.

Cody closed out the theatrical season in 1876 unusually early in response to appeals from officers on the frontier to join them in the upcoming campaign against the nonreservation Sioux bands of Sitting Bull and Crazy Horse. He was reunited with his old friends of the Fifth Cavalry on June 10, 1876, and was immediately reappointed chief-of-scouts by Lieutenant Colonel Eugene A. Carr. Enlisted men as well as officers were delighted to have their old scout back, for when Cody galloped into the camp of the Fifth Cavalry, a cry of "Here's Buffalo Bill" went out, followed by three rousing cheers from the regiment.[48]

"There is very little change in his appearance since I saw him last in '69, except that he looks a little worn, probably caused by his vocation in the East not agreeing with him," noted one enlisted man in a newspaper interview. "All the old boys in the regiment upon seeing General Carr and Cody together, exchanged confidences, and expressed themselves to the effect that with such a leader and scout they could get away with all the Sitting Bulls and Crazy Horses, in the Sioux tribe."[49]

General Sheridan came out to Fort Laramie at this time to in-

[48] Cody, *Life of Hon. William F. Cody*, 340.

[49] Russell, *Buffalo Bill*, 220. Lieutenant Charles King of the Fifth Cavalry met Cody at the train station in Cheyenne and escorted him to the cavalry camp. King later became a prolific author of fiction and history based on his experiences in the Fifth Cavalry, and he left a classic account of the Great Sioux War that features Cody prominently. See Charles King, *Campaigning with Crook* (Norman: University of Oklahoma Press, 1964). For historical overviews of the campaign see Hutton, *Phil Sheridan and His Army*, 282-330; John S. Gray, *Centennial Campaign: The Sioux War of 1876* (Fort Collins: Old Army Press, 1976); Edgar I. Stewart, *Custer's Luck* (Norman: University of Oklahoma Press, 1955); J. W. Vaughn, *With Crook at the Rosebud* (Harrisburg, Pa.: Stackpole Company, 1956); and Jerome A. Greene, *Slim Buttes, 1876: An Episode of the Great Sioux War* (Norman: University of Oklahoma Press, 1982).

spect the Indian agencies on the White River in northern Nebraska. He promptly enlisted Cody to ride with him to Red Cloud
Agency on June 15 to see if reports of Indians leaving the agency
to join Sitting Bull's hostiles were exaggerated. Convinced that
there was no problem at the agency, Sheridan ordered the Fifth
Cavalry north to the Power River Trail, which led from Red Cloud
Agency to the Powder and Yellowstone rivers. The Fifth was to
travel light, scouting westward along the trail in order to block the
retreat of Indians fleeing to the White River agencies. Sheridan
expected columns already in the field under Brigadier Generals
George Crook and Alfred Terry to crush the hostiles; he hoped the
Fifth could block the escape route of the Indians. The Fifth would
also keep a wary eye toward the Indian agencies to stop any rein-
forcements or supplies from reaching Sitting Bull.

The Fifth Cavalry soon learned that it had far more to worry
about than preventing the escape of defeated Indians. On June 17
General Crook's column was attacked by a large force of Sioux and
Cheyennes under Crazy Horse on Montana's Rosebud River and
was forced to retreat. Crazy Horse then turned northwestward to
join Sitting Bull's great encampment on the Little Big Horn River
in time to meet the advance guard of Terry's column, under Lieutenant Colonel George A. Custer. The Indians, numbering between
two and three thousand warriors, overwhelmed the Seventh Cavalry, killing Custer and 262 of his men on June 25.

On July 17, 1876, the Fifth was scouting amongst the rolling
hills along Warbonnet Creek, Nebraska, just south of the Black
Hills of Dakota and just north of the winding Pine Ridge. Near
dawn the advance guard of Little Wolf's Cheyennes, on their way
to join Sitting Bull, clashed with Cody and half a dozen Fifth Cav-
alrymen in a brief skirmish that became one of the most celebrated
incidents of the Great Sioux War. Cody brought down the only casu-
alty of the fight, a Cheyenne warrior named Yellow Hair. As the
remaining Indians galloped away with the Fifth Cavalry in hot
pursuit, Cody dismounted and scalped his fallen foe. "The first
scalp for Custer," he proclaimed, waving the grisly trophy in the
air.[50]

The Fifth chased Little Wolf's people back to Red Cloud Agency
without further incident. The Cheyennes quickly blended back in

[50] Yellow Hair was so named because of a blonde scalp that he had taken. His
name has often been mistranslated as Yellow Hand. The best account of the fight
on Warbonnet Creek is Paul L. Hedren, *First Scalp for Custer: The Skirmish at
Warbonnet Creek, Nebraska, July 17, 1876* (Glendale, Calif.: Arthur H. Clark Co.,
1980).

13. *First Scalp for Custer*, by Robert Lindneux, painted in 1928. While dramatic and colorful, the painting is highly inaccurate and romanticized. The artist seems to have known better than Cody how scouts were supposed to dress and has put the slayer of Yellow Hair back into buckskins.

among the other agency Indians and appeared quite friendly. Lieutenant Charles King, who had witnessed Cody's heroics on Warbonnet Creek, recorded that the Indians were as impressed by Cody as were the whites.

> One and all they wanted to see Buffalo Bill, and wherever he moved they followed him with awe-filled eyes. He wore the same dress in which he had burst upon them in yesterday's fight, a Mexican costume of black velvet, slashed with scarlet and trimmed with silver buttons and lace—one of his theatrical garbs, in which he had done much execution before the footlights in the States, and which now became of intensified value.[51]

The Fifth Cavalry now moved north to reinforce General Crook's column and pursue Sitting Bull's people. Crook now had over two thousand men, and this huge command was designated the Big Horn and Yellowstone Expedition. Buffalo Bill Cody was appointed chief-of-scouts for Crook's command, with some twenty scouts working under him. But as summer faded into August the opportunities for additional action faded as well. The triumphant Indians had scattered, and the lumbering army columns had no chance of catching them. On August 22, Cody asked for his discharge. The opportunity for glory loomed larger as an actor before the eastern footlights than as a scout with Crook's disheartened army.

Cody quickly had a new theatrical combination put together, featuring a companion from the Great Sioux War, Captain Jack Crawford, the so-called poet scout. The new play was entitled *The Red Right Hand; or Buffalo Bill's First Scalp for Custer*. This five-act monstrosity was, according to Cody, "without head or tail, and it made no difference at which act we commenced the performance." Several theater critics were reported to have gone insane attempting to discover a plot. It was just the sort of drama that Buffalo Bill was known for: "a noisy, rattling, gunpowder entertainment . . . [presenting] a succession of scenes in the late Indian war, all of which seemed to give general satisfaction." It was Cody's most successful play.[52]

Not the least of the show's attractions were the scalp and feathered warbonnet of Yellow Hair. When the northeastern press and clergy sent up a howl of protest over this barbaric public display, Cody withdrew his trophies from theater windows and confined

[51] King, *Campaigning with Crook*, 38.
[52] Cody, *Life of Hon. William F. Cody*, 360.

himself to brandishing them on stage. This only increased box of-fice receipts as folks hurried to see the controversial scalp.[53]

Was *The Red Right Hand* a case of art imitating life? Or, rather, had the slaying of the unfortunate Yellow Hair been a case of life imitating art? Cody had, in fact, dressed the morning of July 17, 1876, in one of his stage costumes, a Mexican vaquero outfit, in anticipation of action with the Indians. He wanted to be able to tell his audiences back East that he was wearing an "authentic" scout's costume when he appeared before them. His old buckskins were becoming passé; he needed a brighter, more colorful "authentic" costume. So, dressed properly for the part, he sallied forth and killed an Indian in a grisly ritual that reaffirmed his status as a real frontiersman. Then he hurried eastward, scalp in hand, to ex-ploit the deed. It was as if the frontier West had become a vast living stage, where Cody performed ritualistic acts of heroism for the entertainment of the population of the industrial East. It was a unique moment in time; for the West was providing living, breathing entertainment for the East. By 1876 the frontier was already an anachronism to eastern folk. After his premier perform-ance on Warbonnet Creek, Cody simply took the show on the road. *The Red Right Hand* was a rerun, and the residuals made it quite profitable.

In 1883, inspired by the success of a July 4th rodeo he staged at his North Platte ranch, Cody initiated his famous Wild West show. Cody's outdoor spectacle combined rodeo elements such as bucking broncos, wild steers, roping, and riding with historical motifs from his stage plays such as the Deadwood stage, the Pony Express, and Custer's Last Stand. Various animals from the western wilds were on display, as were famous frontier celebrities such as, over the years, Pawnee Bill, Frank North, Sitting Bull, and, of course, Buffalo Bill. The cowboy, once a pejorative name, now became an American hero in the form of William Levi "Buck" Taylor, the King of the Cowboys, and Johnny Baker, the Cowboy Kid. Displays of marksmanship were provided by Cody, Baker, and most especially Annie Oakley—"Little Sure Shot."

[53] Russell, *Buffalo Bill*, 253-57. The scalp and warbonnet of the unfortunate Yel-low Hair are now on display at the Buffalo Bill Historical Center, Cody, Wyoming. Cody may have been the first, but he was certainly not the last, to comprehend the public fascination with Custer's Last Stand and exploit it. For the evolution of the Custer myth, and Cody's part in it, see Paul A. Hutton, "From Little Bighorn to Little Big Man: The Changing Image of a Western Hero in Popular Culture," *West-ern Historical Quarterly*, VII (January 1976): 19-45; and Brian W. Dippie, *Custer's Last Stand: The Anatomy of an American Myth* (Missoula: University of Montana, 1976).

14. The Evolution of Buffalo Bill: the neophyte thespian, 1873.

Buffalo Bill, the prosperous actor, 1875.

Buffalo Bill, the symbol of the Wild West, 1893.

As time passed Cody updated the historical pageants in the Wild West (he never used the word show) to include events from the Spanish-American War, the Boxer Rebellion, and the Philippine Insurrection. However, events such as an Indian attack on the Deadwood stage and Cody's first scalp for Custer remained standard fare throughout the show's long run.[54]

Cody took his Wild West to London in 1887 for Queen Victoria's Jubilee where it became an international sensation. Buffalo Bill gave the Europeans, just as he had his own countrymen, a taste of the vanishing frontier. He exploited the romantic possibilities of the American West, making them intelligible to millions who would have no other knowledge of the frontier than what he presented. He became a buckskin-clad goodwill ambassador, winning the hearts of the world as no American had done since Benjamin Franklin.

The Wild West show formulated the clichés and conventions later continued in western films and television shows. It fixed Cody in the world's collective imagination as the greatest of the frontiersmen, aided no doubt by 1,700 dime novels featuring Buffalo Bill.[55]

After thirty years of successful operation, in which time Cody made and lost several fortunes, the Wild West show finally failed in 1913. He toured for two more seasons with the Sells-Floto Circus and made his final appearance with Miller Brothers 101 Ranch Wild West in 1916.

William F. "Buffalo Bill" Cody died in Denver on January 10, 1917. It was as if the last connection between the modern America of automobiles, airplanes, and World Wars and the old frontier America of the Pony Express, the stagecoach, and the Indian Wars had been severed. The city of Denver, not about to lose a potential tourist attraction, buried him atop Lookout Mountain in a steel vault lined with concrete. They feared that the citizens of Cody,

[54] The Wild West show is ably and fully discussed in Don Russell, *The Wild West or, A History of the Wild West Shows* (Fort Worth: Amon Carter Museum of Western Art, 1970). Two illustrated books on Cody's show are Isabelle S. Sayers, *Annie Oakley and Buffalo Bill's Wild West* (New York: Dover Publications, 1981); and Jack Rennert, *100 Posters of Buffalo Bill's Wild West* (New York: Darien House, 1976).

[55] A sophisticated and insightful analysis of Cody's role in the creation of the frontier "myth" is in Richard Slotkin, "The 'Wild West,' " in *Buffalo Bill and the Wild West* (New York: Brooklyn Museum, 1981). This lavishly illustrated book was published as a catalog for the traveling exhibit "Buffalo Bill and the Wild West" and contains essays by Peter H. Hassrick, Vine Deloria, Jr., Howard R. Lamar, William Judson, Leslie A. Fiedler, and Slotkin. Also see Dixon Wecter, *The Hero in America: A Chronicle of Hero-Worship* (New York: Charles Scribner's Sons, 1941), 341-63; and Henry Nash Smith, *Virgin Land: The American West as Symbol and Myth* (Cambridge: Harvard University Press, 1970), 102-11.

15. *Buffalo Chase*, by Carl Henckel. After viewing Buffalo Bill's Wild West during one of its Europea[n] tours, Henckel executed a number of drawings of frontier life. The artist, in common with several gene[r]ations of Europeans, visualized the American frontier based on what he saw in Cody's show.

Wyoming, the town Buffalo Bill had promoted and made his home after 1902, might attempt to steal the body. Buffalo Bill was a valuable commodity, dead or alive. The grandiose funeral and steel vault seem somehow fitting. No doubt Cody would have understood. It was, after all, just show business.[56]

[56] The Cody bibliography is vast. High points include the standard biography of Cody, Don Russell's excellent *The Lives and Legends of Buffalo Bill*. Especially useful for its insights into Cody's life at North Platte, Nebraska, is Nellie Snyder Yost, *Buffalo Bill: His Family, Friends, Fame, Failures, and Fortunes* (Chicago: Swallow Press, 1979). A fine pictorial biography is Henry Blackman Sell and Victor Weybright, *Buffalo Bill and the Wild West* (New York: Oxford University Press, 1955). A lavish, beautifully illustrated presentation of the holdings of the Buffalo Bill Historical Center in Cody, Wyoming, is in Margaret L. Kaplan, ed., *The West of Buffalo Bill: Frontier Art, Indian Crafts, Memorabilia from the Buffalo Bill Historical Center* (New York: Henry N. Abrams, Inc., Publishers, n.d.), while a more modest presen-

Buffalo Bill had made a long journey from chief scout at Fort McPherson in 1871 to burial on Lookout Mountain in 1917. The first step in that odyssey was made during General Sheridan's 1871 buffalo hunt. Henry E. Davies, in the following account of that hunt, captures Cody just at the moment of transition between western scout and eastern showman. Davies' description of Cody provides ample evidence of the origins of the larger-than-life figure that would soon be famous worldwide as Buffalo Bill, the greatest showman of his time:

The most striking feature of the whole was the figure of our friend, Buffalo Bill, riding down from the Fort to our camp, mounted upon a snowy white horse. Dressed in a suit of light buckskin, trimmed along the seams with fringes of the same leather, his costume lighted by the crimson shirt worn under his open coat, a broad sombrero on his head, and carrying his rifle lightly in his hand, as his horse came toward us on an easy gallop, he realized to perfection the bold hunter and gallant sportsman of the plains.

---

tation of the holdings of the Buffalo Bill Memorial Museum and Grave in Denver, Colorado, is in O. J. Seiden, *Buffalo Bill—His Life and Legend*, ed. Stan Zamonski (n.p.: Stonehenge Books, 1981).

Cody has had his share of detractors over the years. Two examples of "debunking" biographies are Richard J. Walsh, *The Making of Buffalo Bill: A Study in Heroics* (Indianapolis: Bobbs, Merrill, 1928); and John Burke, *Buffalo Bill: The Noblest Whiteskin* (New York: G. P. Putnam's Sons, 1973).

Members of Cody's family wrote some rather imaginative memoirs. Unreliable but interesting are the memoirs of Cody's wife, from whom he was often estranged: Louisa Frederici Cody and Courtney Riley Cooper, *Memories of Buffalo Bill By His Wife* (New York: D. Appleton and Company, 1919). Cody's sisters also left memoirs. See Helen Cody Wetmore and Zane Grey, *Last of the Great Scouts (Buffalo Bill)* (New York: Grosset & Dunlap, 1918); and Elizabeth Jane Leonard and Julia Cody Goodman, *Buffalo Bill: King of the Old West* (New York: Library Publishers, 1955). A touching memoir by Cody's ward that provides insight into his private affairs is Dan Muller, *My Life with Buffalo Bill* (Chicago: Reilley & Lee, 1948).

Cody's autobiography was published in 1879 by Frank E. Bliss of Hartford, Connecticut. Although critics have suggested that the autobiography was ghostwritten by Ned Buntline or Prentiss Ingraham, internal evidence strongly suggests that Cody wrote it himself. That is the conclusion of the leading authority on Cody, historian Don Russell. Only the first edition of the book, however, is reliable, for it was reprinted in numerous bastardized editions with the addition of much fictional material. The best edition of the autobiography is the 1978 University of Nebraska Press reprint of the first edition (Cody, *The Life of Hon. William F. Cody Known as Buffalo Bill*). It features a useful foreword by Don Russell. Interestingly, Cody dedicated his book to the man whose sage advice set him on the greasepaint road to fame and fortune: General Phil Sheridan.

16. Buffalo Bill bids his audience farewell at the conclusion of his Wild West program, circa 191(

In 1871 young Bill Cody was already playing the role of Buffalo Bill for General Sheridan's dude guests. He was ideally suited for the role, and over the next few years he perfected it to the extent that even he became confused over what was real and what was show business hype. Buffalo Bill became the perfect symbol for America's last frontier, a place where the lines between reality and myth became hopelessly blurred.

TEN DAYS

# ON THE PLAINS

BY

PRINTED BY CROCKER & CO.

NEW YORK.

## To Lieutenant General Sheridan.

General,

To no one could this book be more appropriately dedicated than to yourself for to you alone our party of friends was indebted for all the adventures and enjoyments which it attempts to record.

Your kind hospitality, and generous care for our comfort and welfare, rendered a journey that, under ordinary circumstances, would be trying and difficult, an agreeable and delightful episode in the lives of all who accompanied you; and one which will ever be remembered by us with the highest and warmest appreciation.

I have therefore taken the liberty of dedicating this little volume to you, trusting that notwithstanding its many imperfections you may find in it something of interest or entertainment, and in that hope with the expression of my best wishes for your health and happiness, I remain

Yours, very truly,

\* \*

# TEN DAYS ON THE PLAINS.

# CHAPTER I.

*Invitation to the Hunt—What was expected—Leaving New York*
*—Journey to Chicago—Excitement in the City—The first*
*Buffalo—Dining—Pigeon Shooting, &c.*

LIEUTENANT-GENERAL SHERIDAN, on a visit
to the East during the Summer of 1871, mentioned
to some of his friends that in the month of September he
intended to explore the country between Fort McPherson
on the Platte river, in Nebraska, and Fort Hays, in Kansas,
and kindly invited a large party to accompany him on his
trip. His invitations were gladly accepted, presenting, as
they did, an opportunity of visiting a part of our country
seldom traveled by the white man, and which affords perhaps the best field for the sportsman that can be found in
the United States. What could be more attractive to the
tame citizen of the East than the prospect of traveling in
the wilds of the region we had been taught by our early
studies in geography to describe as the Great American
Desert—to hunt the buffalo, course the antelope, stalk

1

the elk and deer, shoot the wild turkey, and pursue the mighty jack rabbit in his native hills.

The man whose days were passed in the excitements of Wall street could find in the congenial society of buffalo bulls and grizzly bears an agreeable change from the ordinary associations of his life. The sailor could for once desert his accustomed element, and on the great plains of the West form an idea of life on shore that he had never before conceived. The man who had nothing to do could look forward to the prospect of abundant occupation, and he who at his home believed himself to be overworked could imagine in such a trip a period of idleness and ease. Added to all these inducements, there was some slight expectation of becoming acquainted with the noble red man in his own home, and any doubts we had as to the hospitality with which the savage warriors might receive their guests, were dissipated by the assurance that the party would be furnished with a military escort, so strong that if an Indian battle should prove to be one of the entertainments provided for the General's friends, they would be able to return safely to their homes with scalp untouched by a hostile knife, and add to their triumphs as huntsmen the higher glories of successful warriors.

Thus assured, a large and pleasant party was quickly gathered, and the campaign was opened on the evening of the 16th of September, when most of those who intended to participate in the excursion met in a palace car at the Hudson River Railroad Depot, in New York City, *en route* for Chicago, which Gen. Sheridan had fixed as the point of meeting. All came well provided with arms, ammunition and hunting equipments, and due care had been taken to provide amply against all dangers, either physical or spiritual, to which any might be exposed. Old friends shook hands, strangers were introduced and made to feel as friends at once, and at 8 P. M. we were launched upon our journey.

A comfortable car had been secured for our party, and we were provided with every resource to while away the time. The hours passed rapidly and pleasantly, and all felt that the journey had commenced under the best auspices. On the following morning we awoke to find ourselves passing rapidly through Western New York, and early in the day we reached a spot of interest to all of us, the childhood's home of our friend and companion, Mr. Lawrence Jerome. As we passed through the fields so well remembered by him, he held us all absorbed by the anecdotes and incidents of his early career, told in a way to touch every heart; and whenever a stoppage of the train occurred in the towns where he had been known in earlier days, it was affecting to see the interest with which he would rush to the platform of the car and exchange warm and affectionate greetings with his old friends and neighbors. But even for sentiments so touching as his, a railway journey gives but brief time ; and we were carried onward through Buffalo, Cleveland and all the other towns, be they more or less, between New York and Chicago, on the Lake Shore route, until, on the morning of September 18th, on a bright, fine day, we reached Chicago. The Sherman House was fixed upon as our headquarters, and thither we repaired, and soon the large hall of the hotel was encumbered with a pile of gun cases, hunting boots, ammunition boxes, champagne baskets, demijohns and other necessities for a hunting campaign, that astonished and bewildered even the people of Chicago, accustomed as they are to shooting and to drinking at discretion.

A silent and respectful crowd quickly gathered about these objects of general interest, and many and varied were the rumors as to what could be the purpose of these formidable preparations. Some, hearing that one of us wore an Ulster, conjectured that a new Fenian expedition was on foot, forgetting that those brave warriors have always been so thirsty that they invariably consume their spirit rations so far in advance of their objective point that their Dutch courage is never on hand when a campaign fairly begins. Others again, believed that our paternal Government at Washington had at last decided upon actually and openly adopting as its policy, in the settlement of the Indian difficulty, the plan that has unofficially but practically been in use from time immemorial, and that we, as new Peace Commissioners, *vice* Vincent Colyer and others removed, were bound on a mission to the plains to put it in execution. Bibles, moral pocket handkerchiefs, and Quakers having proved to be a failure, it was said that the Government had fallen back upon whisky and gunpowder; and these time-honored remedies for all human ills, coupled with the establishment of a Stock Exchange in the Indian country, were expected to reduce Spotted Tail, Red Cloud and all their brethren to the condition of law-abiding citizens of the United States in the shortest possible time.

The presence with our party of an eminent philanthropist from the City of Brotherly Love gave great strength to the Peace Commission story; and the ingenious author of this theory posted off to a newspaper office to procure the issue of an extra, giving the most reliable and latest intelligence of this strange arrival in the city. He found, however, that he had been anticipated by another news collector, still more ingenious and far more active, who,

without wasting any of his time in inquiry or speculation, had invented, written out and published a complete, exact and veracious account of our party, embellished with incidents, and giving fragments of the personal history of some of us that elevated his paper almost to the dignified position that is assumed by the New York *Sun* whenever that eminent journal has occasion to make mention in its columns of a gentleman.

It was of course gratifying to us, coming from the East, to see that the example of our journalists had been able to influence so powerfully the tone and style of a western paper, and all agreed that our historian required but time and experience to render his paper in all respects a worthy competitor of the reputable journal that he was evidently endeavoring to imitate.

The day in Chicago was spent in making preparations for the trip, purchasing such supplies as our Chicago friends, more versed in western life, informed us were yet necessary to our complete equipment, and in visiting objects of interest about the city. Those who drove to Lincoln Park were gratified by the sight of the buffalo there kept in the zoological gardens, and from the appearance of the undersized dirty brutes that appeared wallowing like hogs in a bed of filth provided by the good citizens of Chicago for their accommodation, our ideas of the majestic and savage animal we came so far to hunt, were materially changed.

One of our most ardent sportsmen offered untold wealth to the policeman in charge of the grounds for the opportunity of taking a few shots at a buffalo, at short range from the outside of the pen, by way of getting his hand in practice, but the guardian of the place, with an appalling indifference to the interests of true sport, turned a deaf ear to his entreaties.

Evening found us seated at a pleasant dinner at the Sherman House, enlivened by the presence of several prominent gentlemen of Chicago, and dinner over, all repaired to General Sheridan's house, where we were most hospitably entertained.

The morning of the following day was spent at the pigeon shooting grounds on Fullerton Avenue, where a closely contested match was shot between Col. Crosby and Mr. Livingston on one side, and Mr. Johnson and Mr. Heckscher on the other.

Mr. Lawrence Jerome, with great kindness, volunteered to undertake the duty of keeping within bounds all pigeons that were missed by the contestants, and performed his task with zeal if not with much success; and General Davies was highly distinguished for the skill displayed by him in keeping the score.

This entertainment was succeeded by a pleasant lunch party at Mr. Johnson's hospitable bachelor mansion on Pine street—a pleasure that can never be renewed, as the scene of our enjoyment was destroyed in the fire that soon after ravaged Chicago.

After lunch a long drive in the environs of Chicago and a visit to the race-track, where a hog show was in progress, occupied the afternoon, and we returned to the hotel with minds overcome by prices of real estate and weights of porkers that could only exist in the enterprising and aspiring West.

A charming dinner at the Chicago Club, given by General Sheridan, closed this day, the last of our stay in Chicago on our outward trip.

## CHAPTER II.

*Our Party—On the Way to the Plains—Journey on the Prairies—Council Bluffs and Missouri River—Omaha—Union Pacific Railroad—The Fat Contributor—The Cups.*

EARLY on Wednesday morning, September 20th, our number was completed by the arrival from New York of Commodore Bennett, of the N. Y. Yacht Club, and at ten o'clock in the morning our party was installed in a spacious palace car on the Northwestern Railroad and fairly started for the plains. And here, as all were first together, is the time to give the muster roll of our expedition, and so their names are given upon this paper to take their place hereafter in history.

Our Commander-in-Chief, Lieut. Gen. Sheridan, comes first, so well and deservedly known to fame, and of whom it is fit here to say that he is as courteous and hospitable as a host, as he is gallant and distinguished as a soldier.

Mr. Lawrence R. Jerome comes next. The gravity, inseparable from advanced years, and official position, were a wholesome and perhaps necessary check on the exuberant spirits of some of the more youthful members of the party; but he was willing to encourage the amusements and sports of his younger friends within all reasonable bounds, and filled, to the satisfaction of all, the part of the heavy father of the expedition.

65

*Mr. Leonard W. Jerome*, who is too well known to require
description.

*Commodore Bennett*, of the N. Y. Yacht Club, and N. Y.
Herald, who had for the time abandoned "his home on
the rolling deep," to try the discomforts of life on shore.

Carroll Livingston, Esq.

Major Heckscher.

Gen. Fitzhugh, of Pittsburg, an old officer of Gen. Sheridan's command during the war.

Capt. M. Edward Rogers, of Philadelphia.

Col. J. Schuyler Crosby.

Gen. Davies.

Samuel Johnson, Esq., of Chicago.

Gen. Stager, Superintendent of the Western Union Telegraph.

Charles Wilson, Esq., editor of the Chicago Journal.

Gen. Rucker, Quartermaster-General, and Dr. Asch,
Surgeon, both on Gen. Sheridan's staff.

Our party thus made up, we left Chicago on a fine bright
morning; intending to go on by rail without a stop, until
we reached Fort McPherson, on the North Platte river, the
point from which our expedition on the plains would start.
Ample provision for all our needs had been made in advance at the Fort, and we would find everything in readiness upon our arrival.

Throughout the day we rode over the rolling prairies of
Illinois and Iowa, scenery that soon becomes monotonous,
but still of interest to those who behold it for the first time;
and which is impressive from the idea it gives by its vast
extent and great fertility of the agricultural resources of
the western country.

A hotel car attached to our train furnished a table that
was far superior to railway refreshments obtainable at the

East, and after a pleasant day, and a sound night's sleep, we rose to find ourselves, on the morning of the 21st, approaching Council Bluffs on the east bank of the Missouri, opposite to Omaha. Here occurred the first interruption to the easy and pleasant course our journey had run since leaving New York.

The rapid and constantly shifting current of the Missouri prevents the building of any wharfs or bulkheads on its banks, and the bridge over the river being incomplete, it took some time and much trouble to place ourselves and all our various belongings upon a dirty ferryboat that conveyed us across the stream.

We reached the city of Omaha after a considerable delay in the crossing, and had time, while waiting for the train that was to carry us further westward, to survey the whole extent of the capital of Nebraska. Everything to make a large city is to be found there, except population, buildings, and the comforts of life. But these slight accessions to the land and to the streets which they have in unlimited quantities, the inhabitants assured us are soon to be provided in abundance.

Though what should induce any human being who can possibly live elsewhere, to go to Omaha, or, having got there, to remain longer than the shortest possible time in which he can get away, is a query that would be difficult indeed to solve. Dealing in real estate seemed to be the chief occupation of the people; everybody had plenty to sell at enormous prices, and if buyers could be found it would doubtless be a profitable business; but still all live in hope that at some time somebody will come to Omaha who will want to purchase. This pleasing anticipation, and the watching of the trains at the railroad, suffice for the employment of the citizens. One gentleman, indeed, was dis-

covered who professed to keep a hotel, but as he had nothing in it to eat, and could give no certain assurance when
there would be anything there that could be eaten, and
was evidently greatly bored by the request made to him
for some kind of entertainment, it was easy to see that he
was a real estate capitalist, who had by some accident got
into his tavern, and had been too lazy ever to take down
the sign.  Some old friends and some new ones were met
among the officers of the army stationed at Omaha, which
is the headquarters of the Department of the Platte, and
who did all that was possible to render our brief stay
pleasant.  About noon we left Omaha on the Union Pacific Railway, and soon found ourselves upon the plains.
Here the road runs for hundreds of miles straight as an
arrow, and flat upon the earth ; without grades to overcome
or rivers to cross.  On either side, far as the eye can
reach, the land spreads out as smooth and level as the ocean
in a calm, and for days the traveler goes on without one
change to break the monotony of the view.  Here and
there at intervals of from ten to twenty miles, a station is
reached, around which are grouped a few small houses
built of boards, and at which five or six people are collected, to witness what is to them the great event of the
day.

One mile of the road is precisely like the other, one
station is the counterpart of the next, and after the novelty
of scene is exhausted it must be confessed that railway
travel on the plains is frightfully monotonous.

However, our party enjoyed the trip well, not being de-
pendent on the scenery alone for interest ; and we were
fortunate in having, as a companion, for some fifty miles
Mr. Griswold, of Cincinnati, who is well known at the
West as a humorous writer for several papers, under the

*nom de plume* of Our Fat Contributor, and a peripatetic philosopher, or, as they are called at the present day, a lecturer, of the school of the late lamented Artemus Ward. His fund of entertaining stories, and the relation of some of his lecturing experiences, told with great effect, made us all regret our arrival at a station where he was obliged to leave the train, being engaged, as he told us, to lecture there that evening. We parted with him with the kindest wishes, including most heartily the hope that he might have an audience, which, judging from the size of the city where he left the train, seemed doubtful. Indeed, to keep him with us, it was proposed to take the whole population on board the train—of which it might have filled half a car—and have him lecture to them while *en route* rather than lose his company. But this he declined, with thanks, and so we parted. How the lecture went off we never heard ; but from the fragments Mr. Griswold gave us there was certainly too much fun in it for the small town in which it was to be delivered, and one could not but pity the few dozen poor people who that evening would be compelled to do an amount of laughing, that should never be imposed on an audience of less than five hundred.

In the afternoon some rode upon the cowcatcher of the engine, others read, and so passed away the time. Evening found us all united in our car, and discussing the prospects of our hunt, so soon to begin. It was agreed that two cups should be procured by general subscription and given on our return, one to him who succeeded in bringing down the first buffalo, and the other to the one who secured the first elk. With conversation and the aid of music the time went by, until we retired at an early hour, expecting to conclude our railway journey during the night

17

## CHAPTER III.

*Platte City—Ride to Fort McPherson—Review of the Troops—
Fort McPherson—Army Life on the Plains—Camp Rucker—
Preparations for the Trip—Buffalo Bill—Choosing Horses—
Ball at the Fort.*

THE next morning, Sept. 22d, we awoke early to find
that our car had been shunted off on a side track
at Platte City during the night, and our travel on the rail
was ended for the time.

Here we were met by Gen. Emory, 5th U. S. Cavalry,
commanding Fort McPherson, who had come over the
preceding evening to meet Gen. Sheridan, and found con-
veyances prepared for our traps and ourselves, to take us
to the Fort after breakfast. We visited the camp of a company of the 5th cavalry stationed at Platte City, for the
protection of the railway, commanded by Major Brown,
who intended to accompany our party on the expedition,
and found the hearty welcome and cordial hospitality that
always is met with among soldiers. A stroll about Platte
City (a proceeding, it must be confessed, that did not take
much time) disclosed little of interest. There were about a
dozen houses—some of boards and some of sun-dried
bricks—the ruins of a good many more ; a few hard looking men, and still harder looking women ; some mules, a
few cows, and a good many goats. Nobody seemed to

18

have any occupation or any means of living, except the
railway employees, and we soon learned that Platte City
was a thing of the past.   It was one of the many towns
called into existence by the building of the Union Pacific
Railway ; that existed, grew, and flourished so long as the
road was incomplete, and the thousands of workmen,
teamsters, and attaches of all kinds required some place
for shelter and some opportunity of spending their money.
It is an old town for that part of the world, and is now un-
dergoing the decline that attends either communities or
individuals that have outlived their usefulness.   Its former
glories were vividly described by an old inhabitant, who
touchingly told how, in the good old days of railroad building, there would be in town each night some five hundred
drunken men with their pockets full of money ; how every
house not devoted to some worse use, was either a drinking shop or a gambling den, and often both ; how never
a night would pass without the pleasing excitement of at
least two murders ; and that always on Saturday evenings
the whole population would vary the usual routine, by a
general free fight, that would furnish the community with
excitement, variety, and conversation until the next occurred.

Whenever the tone of society appeared to be deteriorat-
ing, the majesty of the law would be asserted by the hanging of two or three individuals whom the general popular
sentiment believed could best be spared, and their bodies,
dangling gracefully from a telegraph pole, gave assurance
to all good citizens that if crime existed, somebody was
punished, and the object of an example at least was obtained.

Our western friends upon the plains owe much to the
valuable invention of Morse, for in former times, after

Judge Lynch had caught and convicted (which terms may be taken to be synonymous) a malefactor, it was often a difficult matter to know what to do with him. The total absence of timber interfered greatly with the performance of a dignified and regular execution, and various and often excessively incongruous expedients had to be adopted to put out of the world those gentlemen who were found to be neither useful nor ornamental when alive. Under these circumstances, the crop of people who deserved hanging, but to hang whom no facilities existed, rapidly increased until science and civilization, advancing westward, brought with them the telegraph, and provided the whole continent with a line of gallows arranged about twenty to the mile, for some three thousand miles. The opportunity thus created was speedily improved. But this movement has been somewhat overdone, and a scarcity of subjects for execution is now being acutely felt. Indeed, our cicerone in Platte City told us that there had been but one hanging in a year past, and that fellow was not of much account, and had done nothing in particular to deserve it.

Our meditations over the ruined splendors of Platte City were brought to an end by a summons to breakfast, which we found at the Railway Hotel, and which was cooked and served in a way that could be imitated to advantage in some of our eastern railway saloons. ·

After breakfast we found prepared the carriages to take us to Fort McPherson, distant eighteen miles from Platte City. Gen. Emory's carriage was there, destined for Gen. Sheridan's use. Major Brown turned out a neat phaeton with a very spicy unicorn team, and two four-horse ambulances made up the rest of our transportation, with a couple of army wagons for baggage.

We were soon accommodated in the different vehicles,

19

and started, those who had a fancy to display their skill
as charioteers taking the reins of the ambulances, which
were provided with good teams. The road, though entirely unmade, was excellent, being as hard and smooth as
a turnpike, and in about an hour and a half an eighteen
mile drive was completed, and we came in sight of Fort
McPherson. Here a most unexpected scene was presented.
The garrison, consisting of five companies of the Fifth
Cavalry, under the command of Major Carr, was paraded
to receive Gen. Sheridan, by whom it was to be reviewed,
and to our surprise we found a large party of ladies in
carriages and on horseback, who had been attracted out
to witness the ceremony. It seemed strange to see such
a sight so far as we were from civilization, and in the midst
of such a desert as we were in. The band played, the
cavalry passed in review very handsomely before the General, and we then drove up to the Fort, where Gen. Emory
received us most hospitably, and we were soon presented
to all the inmates of the garrison. A western fort differs
much from the idea conveyed by the word as it is generally used ; and by the term fort is intended a military post
sufficiently protected to be secure against Indian attacks,
but unprovided with artillery beyond two or three field
pieces. Fort McPherson is a large square enclosure (surrounded by a stockade), containing perhaps six acres.

In the interior one side of the square is occupied by the
buildings used as officers' quarters, these being detached
cottages of one story and a half, with verandahs in front,
prettily finished, and, as summer quarters, pleasant enough.
On the opposite side are the men's barracks, long buildings,
each designed to contain a company of troops ; and on the
other two sides of the square are scattered buildings used
for the various needs of the men and officers, such as the
bakery, cook houses, a reading room, and a chapel.

20

21

The majority of the officers were married, and had with them their families, so that something of society could be enjoyed at the post, and all spoke of this Fort as one of the most agreeable stations on the plains. Still, from the interest that was excited by the passing visit of a few strangers, it was easy to see that the life in such a position must be monotonous and dreary in the extreme ; and it was difficult not to pity those—and especially the ladies—whose lives were to be spent in this or in similar garrisons. The officers of a garrison have, of course, occupation, but this is very slight, and offers no variety or interest, except in case they are called upon to take the field, and then they enter upon an Indian campaign, to engage in what are the hardest and most fatiguing duties that in any country soldiers are called upon to undertake—to overcome an enemy whom it is little glory to conquer, and with the certainty of a hideous and repulsive fate in the event of defeat.

To the ladies who are willing to share their husbands' fortunes on the frontier, existence must be dreary indeed. They cannot be said to ever have a home, subject as they are to the constant changes of station required by military discipline ; and while thus cut off from the one sphere in which woman is happy, and always finds interest and occupation, they are deprived of all the amusements and resources that in more favored localities are open to their sex.

However, this was no time to regret the hard fate of our army friends, who, on this occasion, at least, appeared to enjoy themselves highly, and were cordially kind and attentive to the strangers who had entered within their gates.

From the Fort we soon rode down to the place where the camp of our escort had been pitched, and where prepara-

22

tions had been made for our reception, and there found all ready for movement on the following day.

This camp, the first of the expedition, was named Camp Rucker, in honor of General Rucker, Quartermaster-General on General Sheridan's staff, an old and gallant soldier, and with experience as a hunter equaling that he had acquired as an officer.

Everything for our entertainment had been most carefully and completely arranged by Lieutenant Hayes, of the 5th cavalry, who accompanied us as the quartermaster of the expedition, and we found that our expectations of roughing it on the plains were not likely to be realized under his administration. For the use of our party six wall tents had been prepared as sleeping quarters, with one hospital tent to be used as a mess hall and another as a kitchen, and quarters for servants. One hundred cavalry men were encamped about the tents, detailed as an escort, under the command of Major Brown.

A train of sixteen wagons was provided to carry baggage, supplies, and forage, and among them one loaded with ice, the most valuable cargo of all, and which was sufficient to supply our needs during the whole journey.

In addition to the wagons we had three four-horse ambulances to carry guns, and the lighter personal baggage of the party, and in which an opportunity of driving for those who might become weary of the saddle on a long day's march was afforded.

At the camp we were introduced to the far-famed Buffalo Bill, whose name has been lately used to " point a moral and adorn a tale," in the New York Ledger, and whose life and adventures have furnished the material for the brilliant drama that under his name has drawn crowded and delighted audiences at one of our metropolitan theatres.

We had all heard of him as destined to be our guide

across the plains, and had listened to many anecdotes of
his skill and experience as a hunter, and of his daring
bravery and reckless courage as an Indian fighter.   From
these stories the idea had sprung, that in him we should
meet the typical desperado of the West, bristling with
knives and pistols, uncouth in person, and still more disa-
greeable in manners and address.   Instead of all this, it
was a pleasant surprise to find that Buffalo Bill—or, to
name him properly, William Cody, Esquire—which title
he holds of right, being, in the county where his home
is, a justice of the peace, was a mild, agreeable, well-
mannered man, quiet and retiring in disposition, though
well informed and always ready to talk well and earnestly
upon any subject of interest, and in all respects the re-
verse of the person we had expected to meet.   Tall and
somewhat slight in figure, though possessed of great
strength and iron endurance ; straight and erect as an arrow, and with strikingly handsome features, he at once
attracted to him all with whom he became acquainted, and
the better knowledge we gained of him during the days he
spent with our party increased the good impression he
made upon his introduction.

Our first business in camp was to give to each man the
place he was to occupy in the various tents, which were in
number enough to allow three men in each.   This required
some nicety of adjustment, as we had fat men and thin,
short men and tall ; some who snored and some who could
not endure such a habit ; but, at last, all were arranged so
satisfactorily that no change was made throughout the entire trip.   Next in importance came the assignment of
horses.   A number of horses had been provided for our
mounts equal to that of our party, and lots were drawn to
give the preference of choice.   The first choice was won by
Mr. Leonard Jerome, and with excellent judgment he se-

lected a horse that on our long trip proved himself to be the best of the lot.

The horses were drawn off in this way, one by one, some getting good and others poor animals; but the latter, by various exchanges, were substituted for other horses in the garrison, until, at last, every man had a horse with which he expressed himself at least as highly pleased. A pleasant lunch party was given by Gen. Amory at the Fort, made agreeable by the presence of several ladies, and accompanied by music from the excellent band of the Regiment. In the afternoon our horses were tested and ammunition looked over, and some pistol and rifle practice finished the day. At sunset we sat down to our first dinner under canvas, which was warmly commended, and gave promise that we had little to fear from bad living in our campaign, if we should be successful enough with our arms to provide material for our meals.

Our hospitable friends at the Fort, who seemed determined to leave nothing undone that could contribute to our pleasure, during the afternoon sent down invitations for a ball, to be given in the evening, which were, of course, accepted with pleasure.

The large chapel of the Post we found fitted up and decorated for the purpose, the music furnished by the band was beyond praise, our partners were charming and agreeable, and the affair went off with great success. Several supper parties were improvised by some of the officers, who, being unmarried, could venture on a little dissipation, and the pleasant strains of "We Won't Go Home 'Till Morning" were heard about the Fort until a very late hour of the night, to the great prejudice of good order and military discipline. Finally, we left the Fort, and lay down in our tents to sleep for the little time that remained until our preparations for the march in the morning were to be made.

## CHAPTER IV.

*Reveille—Packing Up—Breakfast—Appearance of the Camp—
Buffalo Bill—Starting Out—Company on the March—On the
Plains—Scenery and Characteristics of the Country—Buffalo
Grass—Advantages for Stock Farming—Order of March—
Going into Camp—Dispositions for the Night—No Hope of
Indians—Sheridan's Campaigns—Camp Brown—An Early
Start.*

A T five in the morning a cavalry bugle sounded the
reveille, reminding some, of the old tunes of the
war, with its familiar strains, and giving notice to all that
the time had come to prepare for moving. As we rose,
we discovered that a bed on the ground requires some
practice to be perfectly agreeable, and complaints of stiff
backs and aching bones were heard; but all were soon too
much engaged in preparations for departure to give much
attention to personal discomfort. Immediately after reveille the horses were fed, and the soldiers prepared their
breakfast. With us, as soon as toilets were completed,
packing up began. This done, men of the escort detailed
for this duty struck the tents and began to load the
wagons, while the members of our party took breakfast in
the main tent, which was left standing until the last. This
finished, we were ready for the start on the day's march,
and this routine was followed during every day of the trip.

As is always the case with any body of troops, be it

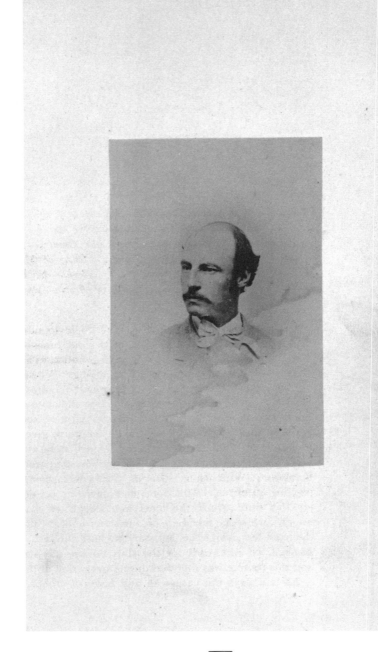

large or small, the first day's march is the most difficult to begin, and many delays occurred while those unaccustomed to camp life and marching, were getting prepared for their move. The scene around our camp was striking and interesting. The rising sun threw his first rays upon the hills that on the South and West surrounded the Fort, and gave just light sufficient to discern the activity and movement in our party.

The white tents, some standing, others upon the ground before being packed, the smoke from expiring camp fires, the movement of the wagons preparing to receive their loads, each with its long team of active, sturdy mules, the soldiers in uniform, some mounted and galloping in different directions upon various errands, and others on foot, all busily engaged, and the various groups of horses, all fresh from long rest and good quarters at the Fort, and seemingly as eager to start upon their journey as the keenest sportsman among us, combined to form a picture at once exciting and attractive, and one that will never be forgotten by those who then beheld it.

The most striking feature of the whole was the figure of our friend Buffalo Bill, riding down from the Fort to our camp, mounted upon a snowy white horse. Dressed in a suit of light buckskin, trimmed along the seams with fringes of the same leather, his costume lighted by the crimson shirt worn under his open coat, a broad sombrero on his head, and carrying his rifle lightly in his hand, as his horse came toward us on an easy gallop, he realized to perfection the bold hunter and gallant sportsman of the plains. With all this to interest and amuse, the time passed rapidly until by half-past seven everything had been done, and mounting our horses, we bade good-bye to Camp Rucker and hospitable Fort McPherson, and started on our journey.

26

27

As we passed the Fort, General and Mrs. Amory, with several of the officers and ladies of the garrison, rode out, some on horseback and some in carriages, and we found they intended accompanying us for the first few miles of our journey, making a very pleasant addition to our company. Our road for ten miles wound through a wooded ravine called Cotton-wood Canon, which intersected the high ground or divide, as it is called, lying between the North Platte and Republican rivers.

With pleasant society, and in the fresh morning air, the first ten miles of our day's journey were rapidly passed over, until surmounting a sharp and long hill, we emerged from the Canon upon the higher ground, and there halted for lunch, and to say farewell to our kind friends from the Fort, from whom we parted with great regret. Their genial hospitality and kind interest for our comfort had made them seem like old friends, and we all retain warm recollections of the pleasant time we passed at Fort McPherson, and the friends we met at that place.

Our adieus made, we turned our faces southward, and moved on towards the place for our camp that night.

After ascending from the ravine, we found ourselves upon the plains, and the scenery was that which we found on each successive day's journey, and which prevails through the whole of this country. The land is intersected by small streams or rivers running almost invariably east and west, along the banks of which are found bottom lands, varying from a hundred yards to a half a mile in width, with a luxuriant soil, suitable for any agricultural use, and generally thickly wooded, with occasional open intervals of meadow, covered with rank, tall grass. The wood found is principally cotton-wood, with some ash, elm, and hickory. From the banks of these streams the ground rises steeply to the height of forty or fifty feet, and then spreads out into a vast plain, undulating to some extent, but rising and falling with a difference of elevation hardly perceptible to the eye.

The plains are intersected by the canons which run generally north and south, and which are abrupt, deep fissures, often miles in length, the sides perpendicular, and ranging in depth from ten to seventy feet. These can be crossed by a mounted man only by the paths made by the buffalo, who, in the course of years, have covered the whole country with trails, and along every canon, at intervals, will be found paths descending one bank, and rising on the other, worn by these animals in their journeyings.

The soil of the plains is composed of a hard, dry clay, in the Summer unyielding to the hoof or wheel, and covered with the buffalo grass, the support of the countless animals that are there found. This grass, short, dry, and nearly yellow in color, at first sight would appear to be incapable of sustaining animal life, but it has been found by experience to be the most nutritious of any of the natural grasses, both for wild and domestic animals. The horses of the Indians, which possess wonderful endurance and vigor, have no other food than this while engaged in the hard marches and rapid journeys they are compelled to take, and, as we were informed by our army friends, remain in good condition under very severe work so long as the grass can be found upon the plains. The cavalry horses brought from the East soon learn to feed upon it, and will prefer it to the higher and more luxuriant grasses of the river bottoms. The game we found was in the best possible condition of high feeding, especially the buffalo, which, except in the case of the very old and feeble bulls, were as fat as domestic cattle in the ordinary condition in which they are sent to market.

This is the country which, but a few years since, was

known as the great American Desert, considered uninhabitable, and impossible to be improved, but which is, in reality, highly valuable, and will in time become the most desirable portion of our country for the breeding of sheep and cattle.  The river bottoms offer eligible sights for settlements, with sufficiency of wood, water, and arable land, while the plains can provide pasturage the whole year round for any number of animals, which would require no care beyond the labor of herding and the construction of shelters to protect them against the bitter winds that occasionally prevail during the Winter.

The elevation of the country, nearly five thousand feet above the sea level, renders the climate bracing and invigorating, and the total absence of swamps and standing water, and the fact that, at such an elevation, evaporation is so rapid that no dew is perceptible, would secure the settler from the malarial fevers that are so prevalent in new settlements further eastward.

Our friends gone, and the country of our travels reached, we settled down into the regular order of marching, which was, with more or less regularity, kept up throughout our journey.   First rode Gen. Sheridan, followed by his guests, and after them the orderlies.  Then came our ambulances, one of which contained a lunch to be eaten in the middle of the day, and which were used from time to time by those who wished a change from horseback riding.  They also contained the spare guns of the party, and in one was carried five grey hounds, brought for coursing antelope and the large rabbits found upon the plains. With the ambulances marched a pair of Indian ponies belonging to Lieut. Hayes, captured during some Indian fight, and harnessed to a light wagon, which Gen. Sheridan occasionally used.  These little horses, but thirteen hands high, showed more vigor and endurance than any other of

the animals we had with us, and during the whole trip were full of life, and as fresh as when starting out. They could climb like cats up and down ravines, with their wagon after them, and few who saw Punch and Judy on the excursion will ever forget these gallant little ponies.

After the ambulances came the main body of our escort, and this again was followed by the supply wagons, all provided with superb mule teams, which had no difficulty in keeping up with the cavalry. Our rate of marching was about five miles an hour, and this always permitted camp to be reached at an early hour, and gave ample time for shooting and hunting after our day's journey was accomplished, in addition to such sport as might be got while on the march.

Our first day's march was not attended with any sport, as no game was to be found near the Fort, and after having made some seventeen miles, we went into camp on the borders of Fox Creek, an affluent of the Republican river.

Our camp was soon pitched on a spot of open ground on the bank of the stream. The horses were picketed with the lariats of their riders, and allowed to graze until evening, when they were brought into the camp, tied up, and fed. The mules unharnessed, were turned loose in a herd, under charge of one of the teamsters, and grazed about the camp until nightfall, when they were also secured. A few sentinels were posted on two or three positions that gave a good view of the surrounding country, and within an hour all our arrangements for passing the night were completed. On the next day we were told we should get into the buffalo country, and the promise of this was sufficient to give to all topics of conversation and interest, and many and various were the questions asked of Buffalo Bill and the others with our party, who were known as adepts in the art of buffalo killing, as to the

28

manner and method of successfully attacking our wished-
for game.

A pleasant dinner closed the day, and in the evening
we gathered about a huge camp-fire, which Gen. Sheridan
had caused to be built in front of his tent, and, seated in
its bright glow, listened to stories of the plains, both of
war and of the chase, and were entertained with excellent songs sung by some gifted amateurs who, fortunately,
were in our party.

We found that none of our hopes of either seeing or
conquering Indians were likely to be gratified. The rigor-
ous peace policy pursued by Gen. Sheridan for the past
two years had proved successful in making the savages
fully understand that a state of war with the government
was to them disastrous, and that he had no belief in the
old policy of bribing them with presents to refrain from
hostilities. Strictly just, and in time of peace a friend and
careful protector of the Indian ; he shows no misplaced
mercy to him in time of war, and the result of his two
winter campaigns has been that now the white man can
travel in safety over the plains, where, a year since, no life
was safe a mile outside the lines of a fort ; and the Indians,
well fed and clothed, are living quietly upon their reservations.

This great result has been accomplished by the General's system of fighting hostile Indians during the Winter.
In Summer, when the grass is fresh and plenty, the Indians,
lightly armed, with no wagon-train, and living entirely on
the game they find in their path, mounted on their ponies,
can always evade and escape from our troops, and for
this reason the campaigns undertaken in the Summer
season have always proved fruitless of result. The Indians
never fight for glory or for success alone ; their battles
must be productive of results in plunder or scalps, and

they will never, if it can be avoided, meet in open combat an enemy who may have even the possibility of triumph; and hence, when traveling is possible, they always avoid meeting our troops when in force. In Winter, however, the positions are reversed, and our troops, with the aid of their supply trains, can travel at a time when the animals of the Indians, from lack of forage, are incapable of movement. This idea was adopted by Gen. Sheridan, and two short Winter campaigns, accompanied by very trifling loss of life, have effectually subdued all Indian hostilities in the vast country that is under his command.

Our evening closed with the christening of the camp, which received the title of Camp Brown, from the name of the gallant officer in command of our escort. Having before us a long march for the following day, and an early start being required, we went to rest at a most virtuous hour, and one that few of us had been accustomed to select as the time for repose for many long years. However, in this case, though it but seldom happens in real life, virtue proved its own reward, and all slept well until a bugle, ringing out at three o'clock in the morning of the 24th, satisfactorily explained to unaccustomed minds the meaning of the words "early start" when used in a military sense.

# CHAPTER V.

*Early Breakfast—Starting on the March—The Buffalo Seen—*
*The First Hunt—Fitzhugh Wins the Cup—Habits of the*
*Old Bulls—Prairie Dogs, Their Habits and Friends—Set-*
*tlement—Elk Hunting—Shooting Buffalo on the March—*
*Crossing the South Fork of the Medicine—Wilson's Elk*
*Wins the Elk Cup—Camp Jack Hayes.*

A BREAKFAST served at half-past four was hardly
tempting until the ingenious idea was originated of
calling it a late supper, under which name it received full
justice.   Before six we were in the saddle, all eager to see
and shoot the buffaloes, which it was certain we should
meet on this day's march.   We soon climbed the high
ground above the little valley in which we had passed the
night, and were again upon the plains and moving rapidly
southward, two or three men being sent on in advance,
with instructions to report back to the main body the first
indications of buffalo that they should observe.

After marching about five miles, we got the welcome
news that buffalo were seen by our advanced guard, and,
after mounting a slight elevation of the ground, six huge
beasts were seen grazing at a distance of about two miles.
The wind blowing directly from us towards the game rendered necessary some precaution in approaching them, as,
unless collected in large numbers, these animals are very

wary, and if they get notice, by scent or sight, of the approach of a hunter, at once take flight; and, unless the pursuer is well mounted and prepared for a long chase, there is little hope of overtaking them. In spite of his great weight and apparently clumsy form, the buffalo has considerable speed, being able to gallop at a rate of ten or twelve miles an hour for long distances, and they never appear to tire out in a chase. They possess, also, great agility in leaping down and climbing up the steep sides of the canons that cross the plains, and often will go over places where a horse is unable to follow them.

After a consultation with Buffalo Bill it was determined that the best mounted of our party should ride through a convenient canon to a distance that would bring them beyond the buffalo, and then, having the advantage of the wind blowing from the animals, ride down upon them. Accordingly, Fitzhugh, Crosby, Lawrence, Jerome, Livingston, Heckscher and Rogers, with Buffalo Bill as guide, started on the hunt, while the rest of us moved slowly forward, keeping behind the crest of a hill that kept us concealed. After a long detour of nearly five miles, our hunters succeeded in getting within two or three hundred yards of the buffalo before they were perceived, and then charged down upon them. The buffalo, as usual, took one good look at their enemies, and then, wheeling around and stretching their tails straight in the air, set off, full gallop, in Indian file, at a pace that tested the best powers of the horses to surpass. Just as they started, our main body emerged from its concealment, and had a full view of the whole hunt, a most exciting and interesting sight to those new to the plains. On came the six huge buffalo, one behind the other, all running together as regularly as if kept in their places by some rule of drill, and close behind them the hunters, each horse doing his best, and now one leading and then another, as though in a hotly contested race. Another moment and a canon is reached, down the steep sides of which the buffalo plunge without relaxing speed, and in an instant are seen climbing the opposite bank. Fitzhugh finds the best place to cross the obstacle, and is seen the first to overcome it, and rapidly catching up with the game, he is alongside the last of the buffalo; in another moment one shot is fired, and the huge brute falters in his step; another, and down he pitches upon his head, nearly turning over and over as he falls. As Fitzhugh pulls up beside his victim, Crosby, on his black pony, shoots by him, and his rifle levels another of the herd; and Livingston, closing up rapidly from the rear, dispatches a third. Those of us not directly engaged in the hunt, pushed up to the scene of action as rapidly as possible, and arrived in time to assist the successful sportsmen in taking the trophies of their hunt. The buffalo hunter always secures the tail of the buffalo he has killed, as the Indian does the scalp of the enemy he has overcome, to prove to the world the fact of his success. The lucky men were heartily congratulated upon their success, and Fitzhugh hailed at once, as the winner of the buffalo cup; while all sympathized with Heckscher, whose chance of killing, at the outset of the chase, was the best of all, but lost, from his horse falling and rolling over him, while descending the bank of the canon. His injuries, fortunately, were very slight, and did not prevent him from keeping the saddle; and he and the other unlucky ones, before the day was done, had opportunity sufficient to make up for any want of success at the outset. The hunt over, we left some men to take out the tongues and best parts of the meat of the buffaloes, and rode on with the column.

We were told, and as the event proved, we should

find buffalo in plenty within the day's march; the finding of a small party of old bulls, such as those we hunted, being always a sign of the vicinity of a herd.

It appears that as the male buffaloes become advanced in life, the younger bulls, as soon as they have age and strength for the combat, combine to drive them from the herd; and these venerable patriarchs, thus excluded from general society, form small clubs among themselves, much as is the custom in civilized life among elderly gentlemen devoted to a life of single blessedness; and, while not daring to mingle with the herds, they keep about the outskirts of the society they once adorned, very much respected, but considered too old fashioned, and too much behind the age to receive attention or consideration. Finding one of these bands of bulls, as they are properly termed, always gives warning that a large herd is near.

The hunt done, and the party collected, we rode forward on our march, our path, for several miles, passing through a prairie dog town, where the ground in every direction was filled with the burrows of these curious little animals. These creatures are found throughout the plains, living together in a sort of society, as thousands of their burrows are found in their so-called towns, adjoining each other, and great care is necessary in riding through these places, the ground being so undermined as often to fall in under the weight of a horse. The prairie dog is a quaint and cunning little creature, somewhat resembling a woodchuck in miniature, and still more like the European marmot. He is from twelve to thirteen inches in length, with a short tail; of a reddish brown color, that at a distance, renders it difficult to distinguish him on the bare earth that always surrounds their burrows. Around the entrance to their holes, the ground is piled up almost a foot high; and on these little elevations, the animals sit upon their hind legs,

and chatter to each other, and observe whatever passes on
the plains. They are very curious, and will watch a passer-
by attentively, and permit him to approach quite near; but
when they have looked sufficiently, they dive into their
holes with wonderful quickness, and with a peculiar toss of
their hind quarters in the air, that defies description. For
this reason, they are difficult to kill, for if hit however
badly, when near their holes, they always succeed in dis-
appearing, and the burrows are so deep and extensive,
that it is the work of hours, to reach the bottom of them
by digging. The only chance of getting them is to hide
near a town, and when the inhabitants are engaged in visiting from one burrow to another, as they constantly do,
when not alarmed by the sight of a man, an opportunity
of knocking them over may be had. In these dog towns
are always found numbers of rattle-snakes, and of small
owls, which live in the same holes as the prairie dogs,
apparently on very good terms, and in a condition of perfect equality. A few of the prairie dogs were killed from
time to time, on our journey, and found very palatable
eating, the meat being much like that of the squirrel. A
short distance beyond the dog town, we met with a settlement situated on a small creek running into the Medicine
river. Here we found five uncivilized white men, each
with a squaw, as a partner of his existence, and each
couple blessed with a numerous family of half-breed children. These people had settled about six months before
on the spot where we found them. Each family lived in
an Indian tent, made of dried buffalo skins, supported on
poles, in shape and size resembling the Sibley tents used
in our army. They owned a herd of horses and mules,
and a few cattle, and had cultivated some portion of the bottom land along the creek, on which they raised corn and
pumpkins, drying the latter for their winter supply of veget-

ables. Their principal occupation was hunting ; and around
the settlement were large numbers of buffalo hides, being
tanned in the Indian manner—removing the hair by soak-
ing in water, and then dressing the skin by rubbing with
the brains and fat of the animal, a process that renders it
exceedingly soft and pliable, and cures it perfectly. We
spent some time in interviewing these oldest inhabitants,
and found that they considered themselves most comfortably and pleasantly situated, and disposed to commiserate
all people so unfortunate as not to be able to live on the
plains, and share the pleasures and delights of the life
they enjoyed. We left these fortunate individuals happy
in their existence, not much superior in comfort or in re-
finement to their next-door neighbors, the prairie dogs, and
soon after reaching the Medicine River, we halted for
lunch. After lunch our party broke into two detachments,
one hunting along the bank of the Medicine River, in the
hope of finding elk or deer, which always frequent the
woods along the streams, and the other remaining with the
main body of the escort. The elk hunters had no success
beyond seeing, and firing a shot in vain after a fine elk that
got away; while the others met buffalo in plenty, and nearly
every one, before the day was over, had killed his first
buffalo.

The most remarkable shot of the day was made by Mr.
Lawrence Jerome, who, while riding in an ambulance, in
the midst of the column, killed a fine bull that attempted
to cross the line of march.

About 4 P. M. we reached the spot for our camp, on the
Mitchell's Fort of the Medicine River, after a long day's
ride, the distance traveled being thirty-five miles in a direct
line, and nearly all of us having ridden at least fifty in the
different excursions that had been made from the route we
followed.

A good deal of time and some trouble were required to pass our teams over to the south bank of the stream, on which our camp for the night was to be established, as a bridge had to be built for the wagons to cross on, and it was necessary to double all the teams to pull up the steep hill that formed the northern bank. At this work, our friend, Buffalo Bill, proved himself as skillful as he was in killing buffalo, and by his science in bridge building, and success as a teamster, acquired new titles to our confidence and respect. At last the day's work was over, and our tents pitched, and all were glad to enjoy the rest that our hard day's ride made so acceptable. On counting our own party at dinner, we found that General Rucker and Mr. Wilson were absent, and on inquiry, learned that they, feeling the day had not afforded them quite enough of excitement, had gone out from camp quietly to enjoy a little hunting by themselves.

Their enterprise and perseverance met its reward; for in an hour, they returned with the news that Mr. Wilson had killed an elk, and soon after, a wagon being sent for it, the animal was brought into camp, and proved to be a magnificent beast, with splendid antlers. Thus Mr. Wilson became the winner of the elk cup, and many were the congratulations that he and Fitzhugh received as being the winners of the two trophies of success in the hunt. By consent of all, the name of Camp Jack Hayes was given to our camp, in honor of Lieutenant Hayes, Fifth Cavalry, who acted as the quartermaster of our expedition, and to whom we all felt indebted, as well for the care and forethought with which our many wants had been provided for, as for his kind assistance and advice in pursuing our sport, and the generosity he displayed in giving every opportunity for success to those not so skilled or experienced as himself. We dined sumptuously this day, having as our *piece de resistance* roast buffalo, and nothing better can be said of it than that it is fully equal to beef, and, indeed, hardly to be distinguished from it.

We sat long this evening around a blazing camp fire, under a cloudless sky, for each one had some story of his own adventures during the day to relate, and slept at last as only men can sleep who have won repose by a day of the hardest work.

# CHAPTER VI.

*In the Buffalo Country—Shooting Buffalo—Coursing Antelope
—How they are Shot—Camp on the Republican—Wild Tur-
keys—Elk—Deer—Camp Asch—Fording the Republican—
Large Herd of Buffalo—Loss of Buckskin Joe—Camp on the
Beaver—Abundance of Game—Camp Cody.*

GENERAL SHERIDAN had some compassion on our
tired condition, and on the morning of the 25th,
reveille sounded at the very reasonable hour of six, and
we broke camp and moved off at eight.

We had reached the country where buffalo were to be
found in abundance, and hence we had no further reason
for haste in traveling, it being our intention to make short
marches while in the country where game was plenty, and
have opportunity for hunting away from the line of march.

This morning our party broke into three detachments—
one in charge of Lieutenant Hayes, going to the right, another, with Buffalo Bill as guide, bore off to the left, while
a few, remaining with the wagons and troops, proceeded
on the direct line to our next camping ground.

Those who were with the wagons had a good day's sport,
buffalo being plenty, and many running across the trail we
were traveling  One party of eight crossed our path
about two hundred yards in advance of us, and gave General Sheridan an opportunity of testing the value of a new

gun he had with him of the Ward Burton pattern. With two shots he knocked over the two leading animals of the herd, killing each dead with a single shot. Three others in the party each killed his buffalo out of this band. Soon after an antelope was seen, and we attempted to catch it with some of the dogs we carried in the ambulance. A fine English grayhound bitch, imported by General Sheridan, and a hound belonging to Major Brown, were started, and we had the view of a very exciting chase, as the antelope ran in a circle for a long time within our sight. It tired out the dogs at last, and got off clear.

This was an invariable experience in coursing the antelope with dogs. We had several grayhounds as good as could be procured in this country, and the bitch, owned by Gen. Sheridan, was of the best English thoroughbred stock, yet, in no instance, did they succeed in taking an antelope : these little animals, possessing immense speed and endurance, far exceeding that of the hounds. Quite a number were shot during the trip, by stalking them on foot, and, with a little patience on the hunter's part, they are easily killed.

It is a remarkably inquisitive creature, and if not at first alarmed, will gradually approach any object to which it is unaccustomed. When an antelope is seen, if the hunter will remain perfectly quiet and motionless, and is to windward of his game, the antelope will move from side to side watching him, and by degrees coming nearer and nearer, until an excellent opportunity for a shot is had.

We reached the junction of the Republican and Medicine Rivers soon after our antelope hunt, and completed there an easy day's march of but thirteen miles, getting into Camp about one P. M.

The party with Lieutenant Hayes had excellent sport. They met a flock of wild turkey about three miles from our late camp, of which Mr. Heckshcher killed the first. Mr. Livingston was so fortunate as to bring down two with one bullet, and General Fitzhugh killed two. They killed several buffalo, among them a magnificent bull, the credit for which was divided between Livingston and Heckscher; four prairie dogs and two antelopes—one of the latter shot by Lieutenant Hayes and the other by Heckscher. The third detachment of sportsmen had equal good fortune. Mr. Johnston killed a black-tailed deer. General Stager stalked and killed an elk, and an orderly with the party killed a second. Mr. Lawrence Jerome in the morning, by the exercise of his unrivalled powers of persuasion, succeeded in obtaining from Buffalo Bill the best hunting horse in the whole party—a dismal looking, dun-colored brute, rejoicing in the name of Buckskin Joe; but, like a singed cat, much better than he looked. He was a wonderful beast for hunting, as his subsequent conduct proved, and on his back Jerome did wonders for one brief day among the buffalo. Leonard Jerome, Bennett, and Rogers were all successful in hunting buffalo, and evening found us collected in camp around our dinner table, all contented with the fortune the day had brought. General Sheridan had tried his luck at fishing during the afternoon, and succeeded in catching fourteen fish, of a kind unknown at the East, called cisco—something like perch, which we found were excellent for the table.

Our camp of this night was named Camp Asch, to commemorate our surgeon, Dr. Asch, of whose professional skill nothing can speak more highly than the fact that not one of us had any ailment whatever while under his care, assisted as he was by Mr. Heckscher, who, on several occasions, displayed eminent ability as an amateur doctor.

Before reveille on the morning of the 26th, we were awakened by two shots, which proved to be from Mr. Wil-

son, who had killed two fine mallard duck that were flying
over the camp.

We left camp about 8 A. M., and forded the Republican
River at the beginning of our march. This stream is
quite wide, but very shallow during the Summer ; the banks,
however, showed that it was subject to heavy freshets
in the Spring, when it must obtain considerable size.
About two miles south of the river we came upon an immense number of buffalo scattered over the country in
every direction, as far as the eye could reach, and all had
an opportunity for as much buffalo hunting as they
wished. The wagons and troops marched slowly along in
the direction of our next camp, while the hunters went off
separately or by twos and threes in different directions,
and all were successful. Lawrence Jerome, mounted on
his charger, Buckskin Joe, and envied by all for having so
good a mount, was doing his utmost when his career was
brought to an untimely end. He had dismounted to take
a particularly careful shot at a buffalo he wished to secure,
and incautiously let go of his horse's bridle. The buffalo,
contrary to rule, running off at the shot, instead of drop-
ping as he was bound to do, was followed by Buckskin
Joe, determined to do a little hunting on his own account,
and perhaps wishing to show Mr. Jerome how the thing
should be properly done. His master watched the chase
with great interest, and the last seen of Buckskin Joe, he
was a little ahead of the buffalo, and gaining slightly,
leaving his rider to his own reflections and a tramp of
some distance, until his desolate condition was discerned,
and another horse sent him, warranted not to run under
any provocation.                                          31

It may be added here, that three days after his desertion
of our party, as we subsequently learned, Buckskin Joe,
all saddled and bridled, turned up a Fort McPherson,

where he still remains in the service of his country. After a pleasant march of fifteen miles, we reached camp on the bank of the Beaver River, in a charming spot, and were soon most comfortably established. The region about the Beaver River was in former times the choicest of the Indian hunting grounds, abounding, as it does, in game of all kinds, and being well watered and provided with timber. Along the banks of the stream for many miles were found the remains of what had once been Indian Camps, in the days when the Indians were the undisputed masters of this country. Nothing could be more attractive to the hunter than this ground. The plains were covered with buffalo; in the low grounds, about the banks of the river elk and deer were plenty, antelopes and rabbits were found in all directions, and turkeys and wild ducks were abundant.

It was determined to remain over a day in this camp, as this was the best hunting ground we could find on our trip. In the afternoon, some hunted for turkeys and ducks, which were got in numbers, and the evening found us as usual. The camp was named Camp Cody, after our guide, philosopher and friend, Buffalo Bill.

## CHAPTER VIII.

*Day at Camp Cody—Porcupine—Hunting Jack Rabbits— Coyotes—Elk, Antelope, Wild Turkeys—Dinner—Court-Martial.*

ON the morning of the 27th we enjoyed the comfort of a late breakfast, and having no march to make, could take as much time for the meal as the most luxurious among us thought desirable. While at breakfast an addition was made to our party by the arrival in camp of a porcupine, which some of the men had caught at a little distance from camp, and brought in by the aid of several halter straps fastened about him. It was a very large and fine animal of the kind, and a box being made for him, was accepted at once as a companion of our journey, with the intention of bringing him to New York upon our return. Our hospitality and attention were, however, thrown away upon the creature, for two nights afterward he contrived to gnaw away some of the bars of his cage, and, turning his back upon the blessings of civilization and improvement so liberally offered, he escaped to his native plains to pursue his former inglorious and barbarous existence.

After breakfast our party, in small detachments, went in different directions to seek such fortune as chance might throw in our paths.

Gen. Sheridan took with him the grayhounds, and, with his companions, had some excellent sport in coursing the jack rabbits that were found in numbers about our camp.

These animals are called the jack or jackass rabbits, from the size of the ears, which are nearly six inches in length ; but they are properly a species of hare. Their habits are those of the latter animal, and except in color and the excessive length of ear, they much resemble the English hare. When alarmed, they at first sit up on their hind legs until they can get a view of the enemy, and then make off at great speed, frequently turning and doubling as they run; and their speed is so great that it required the best efforts of our choicest dogs to overtake them. They have a singular habit while running of occasionally rising on their hindlegs and making a dozen leaps after the manner of a kangaroo, and then resuming their usual method of going.

After getting several rabbits, two coyotes, or prairie wolves, were seen, and the dogs started in pursuit of them. They ran well, but were no match for the dogs, who soon overtook and attacked the slower of the two, upon which the other turned and came back to aid his comrade ; and they fought most savagely until a pistol shot from one of the orderlies gave each his quietus.

These prairie wolves were our constant attendants on the whole march, following us at a distance sufficient to preserve them from any chance of a shot, and feeding upon the remains of any game that might be left behind. At night they always gathered about our camp, and kept up, as long as the darkness lasted, a chorus of the most fearful and mournful howls. Utterly worthless for any other purpose, they are of some service as scavengers of the country, and a buffalo killed over night, and left on the

32

plains, will be found on the following morning to be entirely devoured, and the bones as cleanly picked as if prepared for a specimen.

General Fitzhugh, on the banks of the stream next south of the Beaver, killed an elk whose head and antlers, the finest we had obtained, he carried home as a trophy.

Crosby killed an antelope during the day, and Dr. Asch and General Stager were very successful in shooting wild turkeys.

Our attendants having the day before them undisturbed, had made great efforts with the dinner; and with the appetites of hunters, we did credit to their exertions. Traveling as we were, we were obliged to depend for support upon our skill as marksmen, and the dinner of the day is given here to show the privations that all who determine to dare the perils of a trip on the plains must put up with:

SOUP.

Buffalo Tail.

FISH.

Cisco broiled, fried Dace.

ENTREES.

Salmi of Prairie Dog, Stewed Rabbit, Filet of Buffalo, aux Champignons.

ROAST.

Elk, Antelope, Black-tailed Deer, Wild Turkey.

BROILED.

Teal, Mallard, Antelope Chops, Buffalo-Calf Steaks, Young Wild Turkey.

VEGETABLES.

Sweet Potatoes, Mashed Potatoes, Green Peas.

# COURT MARTIAL.

### DESSERT.

Tapioca Pudding.

### VINS.

Champagne Frappe, Champagne au Naturel, Claret, Whiskey, Brandy, and Bass' Ale.

### COFFEE.

On such simple, hardy food as this we were compelled to live, and yet all had appetite and thoroughly relished their hunter's fare.

This evening was made memorable by a painful duty that had for some time past been pressing itself upon our attention.

One unfortunate member of our party had committed many offences that had passed for awhile unpunished, all hoping that good associations around him, and the many excellent examples constantly before his eyes, would check him in his fatal course, and that an awakened conscience would alone suffice to bring him back to the paths of virtue and rectitude. But these had no effect, and in the interests of discipline and good order, it was, to the great regret of all, found needful that more serious measures must be taken.

A court-martial was therefore organized, and before the august tribunal the unhappy man was brought and held to answer.

The prosecuting officer, obliged by stern duty to pursue his task, detailed before the judges the hideous story of the wretched criminal's offences, and supported his case with the most positive and direct testimony that remained unshaken after a severe cross-examination.

It was clearly proved that the criminal had aided and abetted in the loss of a Government horse ; that there was

112

strong reason to believe he had something to do with the
mysterious disappearance of a Colt's pistol, which he had
borrowed from its owner, and which had never since been
seen; that there was no doubt of the fact that he had felo-
niously disposed of several pocket-pistols, the property of
others; that at night he snored in a manner that was fiend-
ish, and, in addition to all this, he had been guilty of a variety of other less offences too numerous to mention.

The unfortunate prisoner, after a feeble attempt to evade
the charge in reference to the Colt pistol, by stating that
he had returned a horse-pistol to the party owning the
weapon, and claiming that instead of losing a Government horse, the fact was that the horse had lost him; in
both of which defences, it is needless to say, he failed entirely, made a futile effort to prove good character, and
finally, confessing all, threw himself upon the mercy of the
Court.

Chief Justice Cody delivered the opinion of the Court
in a manner at once dignified and able, and as an act of
clemency, suspended judgment for the time being, remark-
ing, that while the camp fire held out to burn the vilest sin-
ner might return, and in hope of amendment, he would
defer sentence.

This impressive exhibition of justice concluded, all returned to rest, sadder and wiser men.

# CHAPTER VIII.

*Early Start—Crossing the South Beaver—Camp on Short-Nose Creek—Buffalo, Turkeys—Party Lost—Camp Stager—March to the North Solom n—Beaver Dam—Camp Jerome—Helping the Mules—Interesting Relics.*

A PORTION of the command made a very early start on the morning of the 28th, thirty men, under Lieutenant Hayes, being sent forward nine miles to the South Beaver River, to prepare a crossing place for the main body, which was to leave camp at the usual time.

Two very enthusiastic hunters rose at three o'clock to accompany this party, but gained nothing but one ante-lope by their diligence.

The crossing of this stream, even after our preparations, was found a difficult undertaking, and nearly two hours were occupied in getting over. After crossing, we found a very fair road, and marching rapidly forward we reached camp on the Short-Nose Creek about 2 P. M., after a march of twenty-four miles.

After making camp, some buffalo were seen about a mile away ; and the afternoon was spent in hunting them, and shooting turkeys. Of the latter General Sheridan got five, a very good bag of this game for one afternoon. Colonel Crosby, with Livingston and Heckscher, had parted with us at the crossing of the South Beaver, intending to keep to our right on the march, and as they did not come in for a long time after we were in camp, some fear was felt lest they might have lost their direction, but, about six in the evening, they turned up all right, with a number of turkeys and ducks, after a very long ride, and after feeling some apprehension that they had mistaken their way, and might have to camp out on the plains all night. Nothing is easier than for a traveler, not accustomed to the plains, to lose the direction of his journey, and, once bewildered, it is scarcely possible to again get on the right track unassisted. Some of the men with us had had the experience of being lost, and say that a man once turned wrong will generally travel in a circle of greater or less dimensions, and there is very little hope of his ever finding his way, unless he, fortunately, should strike a trail or get within sight of some landmark that can indicate his route. Of these aids to travel there are, of course, but very few to be found on the plains. The different streams resemble each other so closely that they cannot be distinguished by an inexperienced eye, and there are few hills or prominent elevations that present individuality sufficient to attract observation, or remain fixed in the memory.

It is never safe, while on the plains, to stray far from the party with which one travels, and though at present there is not much to apprehend, when lost, beyond discomfort and privation, it is not at all desirable to run the risk of those inconveniences.

As the sun went down the weather became very cold, but a good dinner and a bright camp fire made us indifferent to this, and the evening passed jovially in our camp, to which the name of Camp Stager was given, with the full consent of all.

On the morning of the 29th we got off at seven A. M.,

and traveled rapidly for twenty-four miles until we reached
our halting place, on the North Solomon River, about one
P. M.

We found the freshest and clearest water that we had
seen during our march in this river, which flows over a
clear sandy bed, and gave opportunity for a refreshing and
welcome bath.

Our account of game for this day was not large, com-
pristng only three buffaloes, two antelopes, two raccoons,
and three teal ; and we found that, as we went southward,
we were leaving the best hunting grounds.

Near our camp was a large beaver dam, which was well
worth seeing, it being the largest structure of the kind we
had met in our journey.   The beaver had selected for the
place of their work a spot a little distance below the junction of two streams, where they secured an abundant
supply of water, and having built a dam some six feet high
and twenty yards wide, they had made a pond covering
more than four acres.  The ground all around was covered
with the evidences of their labor, shown in the stumps of
the trees and filled with the chips they had bitten out in
gnawing down the trees, and the small limbs and brushwood
they had lopped from the timber used.  Many cotton-wood
trees, eighteen inches in diameter, had been cut down and
used in the construction of the dam, and we found several
upon which they had been working when disturbed by our
approach.  We looked long and anxiously to get some
view of the animals themselves, but without success ; and
were told by the old hunters in our party that the beaver is
so cautious and wary that it is scarcely ever possible to
get sight of them.   They can only be taken in traps, and
then the greatest care is required to obtain them.

Our camp of this evening was distinguished by the
name of Camp Leonard Jerome, and its godfather ex-

tended the hospitalities of his new possession in a most satisfactory manner, and won the highest praises of his guests at an impromptu entertainment he gave.

Our teams had begun in some degree to feel the toil of their march, and we saw that it was the part of true humanity to relieve them as much as possible, and, therefore, every one felt it his duty on this, and on the few remaining evenings of our trip, to lessen the burdens of these unhappy animals by a generous and rapid consumption of our stores.

With this worthy object in view, all applied themselves to the good work with a zeal that would have won the applause of Mr. Bergh could he but have witnessed it, and that no doubt, would entitle some to the medals bestowed by the amiable society over which he presides, if their unselfish labors had been presented to it in a proper light.

However, the want of appreciation did not relax our exertions, and the mules and ourselves, if no others, were much benefitted by the work of the evening, and, doubtless, the antiquary of some thousands of years hence, if he should explore the site of Camp Jerome, will find convincing proof that the primitive man, whose traces he will be searching for, used black vases, with long and narrow necks, marked Mumm and Roederer, the uses and purposes of which will afford a fertile field for the speculations of the savans of that day.

# CHAPTER IX.

*Little Game—Camp on the South Solomon River—Accident to Hound—Bill's Ride to Fort Hayes—Camp Sam Johnson's March to the Salina—Buffalo Hunt—Arrival of the Mail—Camp Davies—Disturbances in Camp.*

THE morning of the 30th was clear and bright, and at our usual hour we started for the day's march. A very heavy wind prevailed all day, blowing with a force that is experienced only at sea, or on the vast, unbroken plains of the West. We found no game except a few buffalo during the day until our march had been completed, when a good flock of turkeys was started in the woods on the banks of South Fork of the Solomon River, where we halted, after having made twenty-five miles. Nine of the turkeys were shot, which, with two rabbits and three or four buffalo, were all the game obtained that day.

In the evening an accident happened to Gen. Sheridan's grayhound, which, while coursing a rabbit, ran against and almost impaled herself upon a sharp, projecting limb of a tree that had been cut down, running the wood more than three inches inches into her chest. The valuable service of our medical staff were at once called into requisition, and the piece of wood being extracted, the poor dog was carefully tended, and, as we afterwards learned, in a month recovered entirely from the wound.

We were now but forty-five miles from Fort Hayes, the point at which we expected to strike the Kansas Pacific Railway, and when our journey on the plains would end; our friends in Chicago had promised to forward all letters for our party to that point, and Buffalo Bill on this evening volunteered to ride into Fort Hayes, and meet us on the next day, bringing with him all the letters that might be at the post.

Taking the best horse that was with the command, he started on a dark night, expecting, as he said, to reach Fort Hayes in about four hours from the time he left us.

Our camping ground will hereafter rejoice in the name of Camp Sam Johnson, a name bestowed for the reason that " he was a jolly good fellow," which was forcibly and at great length insisted upon during the evening by the musical members of our party, in the intervals of our efforts to reduce the excessive amount of stores still found in the wagons.

The next morning, that of October 1st, found us early on our way, and with little to commemorate, we traveled thirty miles until the Salina River was reached, where we made our last camp on the plains. Just as we reached the river some buffalo and antelope were seen, and several of the former killed. While hunting these, Fitzhugh had a narrow escape of being unhorsed : a buffalo cow, that he had wounded, making a desperate charge at him, and just grazing his horse's flank with her horn. In this place let it be said, for the information of all future novel writers who undertake to depict stirring scenes upon the plains, that it is from cows and not from bulls that any danger to the hunter is to be expected. The cow is much more active, spirited, and malicious than the bull, and will make a much harder fight than the latter, who permits himself to be killed with great equanimity, and little, if any, remonstrance.

As we were engaged in this, as it proved our last hunt, we were agreeably surprised to see Buffalo Bill in the middle of the herd, engaged in killing a young buffalo, which he soon accomplished, and then joined us, bringing with him a large mail that he had found at Fort Hayes, which afforded to us all welcome reading matter upon our arrival at camp. We passed a quiet afternoon, and in the evening gathered around our camp fire for the last time. The duty of naming the camp, which was called Camp Davies, having been duly performed, the different members of our party joined in an effort to make that night the pleasantest of all we had spent together, and as it was agreed upon all sides with great success. We had eloquent speeches, melodious songs, and interesting anecdotes, accompanied with a potent incitement to jollity in an immense reservoir of champagne punch, most excellently made, and until a late hour the coyotes, and any other neighbors we might have had, were listening in suspense to these unaccustomed sounds that awakened the echoes along the banks of the Salina. Even after all had retired, the adventures of the night were not over; in one tent a lively rattlesnake prevented for some time the slumbers of its occupants, while another tent, in consequence of insecure fastenings, or some cause unascertained, fell gently to the ground, deserting its inmates, whom it should have protected, but who, in guileless innocence and peace, slept sweetly through the night, all undisturbed.

A story was told the next day, that, while our camp was buried in repose that night, a small party of Indians roamed among the sleepers, and the appearance of an undersized and ill-favored little squaw, dressed in a complete suit of red flannel, who accompanied the chief in command of the party, was minutely described by those who pretended to have observed these unexpected and unwelcome visitors. The story, though told so circumstantially by those who claimed to have seen what they related, was not believed, and it was generally supposed to have resulted from the stimulating effects of punch acting upon minds morbidly excited by some terrific stories of Indians, and their ways and manners, that Buffalo Bill had narrated during the evening.

33

## CHAPTER X.

*Arrival at Fort Hayes—Camp Heckscher—Start for the East—
Chicago Again—Presentation to Lawrence Jerome—Break
up of the Party.*

ON the morning of the 2d we marched to Fort Hayes,
distant but fifteen miles, seeing no game upon the
way. On reaching the post, which is near the railroad,
we pitched our tents once more, expecting to remain in
camp another night, while waiting for a car that had been
telegraphed for to receive our party, but soon learned that
it had been already sent forward in anticipation of our
arrival, and that we could start for the East at three
o'clock by attaching our car to a train that would pass at
that hour. We had received here, through the kindness
of General Stager, telegraphic dispatches of all that was
going on in the world at large, and the alarming news we
had of a panic in the financial world made some of our
capitalists extremely anxious to return home. This, however,
was fortunately proved by later dispatches to be a mistake,
and the minds of such as had any money to lose were agreeably relieved. We also learned here, for the first time, of
the changes that had so suddenly occurred in the City
Government of New York, and this making perceptible

the great need that existed in that unfortunate city, at such
a crisis, for the presence of its purest and best citizens was
35    a strong motive to induce our speedy return.

It was, therefore, unanimously voted to take the train
that afternoon, and after exchanging our hunting equipment for the clothes of civilized life, and duly christening
Camp Heckscher, the last of our homes under canvas,
we proceeded to the depot to embark for home.

Here we parted with Major Brown and Lieutenant
Hayes, who were to return in a few days to Fort McPherson with the wagons and troops, regretting much to lose
them from our party, and recognizing most sincerely the
obligations we were under to these officers for their pleasant society and their kind and successful efforts for our
comfort and enjoyment on the trip. Here, also, we all
shook hands and exchanged a hearty good-bye with Buffalo
Bill, to whose skill as a hunter, and experience as a guide,
we were so much indebted.

We found a comfortable and pleasant car reserved for
our use, and in a few moments we were speeding Eastward, with nothing left us of our life of the past ten days
but pleasant memories and the trophies of success that
we had secured.

Our journey back to Chicago was pleasant, but un-
eventful, and we reached that city after an easy
and comfortable journey on the morning of the fourth of
October.

After the performance of the duties of the toilet, required upon returning to domestic life from so long a
sojourn in the wilderness, including the sacrifice of several
very promising beards, we all met around a well-spread
breakfast-table, at the Sherman House, in company with
several of our friends residing in Chicago, and passed the
morning pleasantly in recalling the incidents of the trip

and in relating the various fortunes that attended the different members of our party.

A very interesting circumstance of this entertainment was the presentation by the guests of a testimonial to Mr Lawrence Jerome, in recognition of his powers as a hunter, and of the high esteem in which he was held by all.

This consisted of a magnificent cane, made of a growth peculiar to the plains, handsomely mounted and adorned with an appropriate inscription. It was accepted by its recipient with great emotion, and in eloquent and fitting words, he told us of his grateful appreciation of the gift so unexpectedly conferred, and of the tender regard with which he would always cherish the present, and remember those by whom it had been bestowed.

Our party was again that evening brought together at an elegant dinner given by General Stager at the Chicago Club, and which was most highly and deservedly enjoyed, and with this last feast the history of our party on the plains comes to an end.

The next day saw most of us on their way to their respective homes, and almost upon our arrival we all were shocked to learn of the great calamity that so shortly after our departure overwhelmed the hospitable and pleasant city in which we had passed such joyous days, and of the misfortunes that had overtaken the kind friends we left there but a few hours before in the enjoyment of all that can make life happy. Fortunately for them, the same spirit and enterprise, that had so rapidly and marvelously built up the city of their homes, still survive ; and we hear with pleasure that a new Chicago is rising upon the ruins of the old that bids fair to surpass the city of which we retain such pleasant memories.

36

The writer here has reached the end of a narrative that, at the request of his companions of the hunt, he undertook. This duty was assumed with some reluctance, by one who has never before ventured to trust to the criticism of the world any efforts of his pen, and this would not have been undertaken but for the fact that it is intended for circulation only among those whose interest in the scenes described, and in the story told, will prevent them from looking upon it with the uninterested and impartial eye of the ordinary reader of such a narrative.

Comrades of the hunt and of the bivouac, it is hoped, will look upon this only as an attempt well meant, however it may have been accomplished, by one of their number to tell simply and truthfully the incidents and events of a journey that was delightful while it continued, and will ever be grateful in memory. In writing it out there has been much that was gratifying, for as every scene and every event of those pleasant days have been set down, they almost seemed in reality to return again ; and if any reader shall derive from these pages the same enjoyment that has accompanied their preparation, the writer's aim will have been more than accomplished, and his labor will have received the highest reward he could have asked.

While the end is reached, it is yet difficult to pen the final word, and to know that written, our hunt, and all belonging to it, is at an end. No party of the kind could have been more pleasant, more harmonious, or more happy. It is hard to feel that such associations and such enjoyments are of necessity but short in duration and infrequent in occurrence, and still harder to think, that in all human probability, the band of friends, who so long rode, hunted and feasted together on the wide Western plains will never again be united as they then were. With the kindest wishes to all, and with pleasantest memories of the past, the story of the hunt is concluded.

THE END.

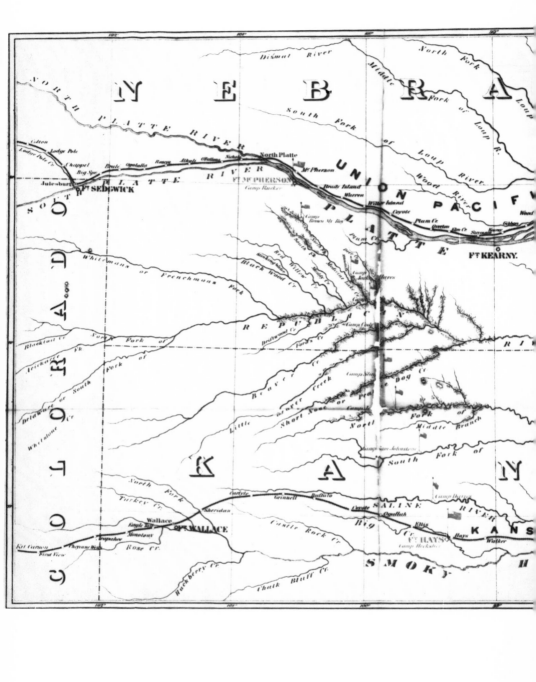

# MAP
## SHOWING TRAIL OF
## GENERAL SHERIDAN'S
## GREAT BUFFALO HUNT.
### SEPT. & OCT. 1871.

**Scale.**

Drawn in Engineer Office
Hd. Qrs. Mil. Div. of the Missouri

Capt. Corps of Engineers U.S.A.

| Distances. | |
|---|---|
| 1st day | 49 Miles |
| 2 " | 38 " |
| 3 " | 17 " |
| 4 " | 16 " |
| 5 " | 0 " |
| 6 " | 20 " |
| 7 " | 22 " |
| 8 " | 18 " |
| 9 " | 25 " |
| 10 " | 10 " |
| Total | 194 Miles. |

# NOTES

1. Sheridan was actually returning to the United States from Europe, where he had been an observer with the Prussian army during the Franco-Prussian War. Upon his return, after almost a year observing the conflict as well as touring Europe and the Middle East, he visited President Ulysses S. Grant at the fashionable resort of Long Branch, New Jersey, where the President had a summer home. It was there that Sheridan met several of the young men of high society whom he invited to join him on an autumn buffalo hunt.

2. Vincent Colyer was secretary to the Board of Indian Commissioners, a civilian organization made up of leading philanthropists appointed by the President to work with government officers in the disbursement of funds for the Indians and to give advice on Indian affairs. Founded in 1868 as part of President Grant's so-called Indian Peace Policy, the board had already been involved in several disputes with government officials and army officers over Indian affairs. One of the most heated of these debates had occurred between Colyer and General Sheridan over the slaughter of a band of Piegan Indians on Montana's Marias River in January 1869. Colyer was a highly respected humanitarian, a leader of the YMCA, former secretary to the U.S. Christian Commission during the Civil War, and a member of Peter Cooper's U.S. Indian Commission. His charge that the slaughtered Indians had been peaceful was entirely correct and so discredited the army that an attempt to transfer control of Indian affairs from the Department of the Interior to the Department of War failed to pass in Congress. Colyer's high visibility made him a handy whipping boy for frustrated army officers, and Sheridan, who could readily handle a whip, accused the secretary in 1870 of "deceiving the kind-hearted public . . . to further

the end of the Indian Ring, doubtless in whose interest he is writing." The "Indian Ring," according to Sheridan, had "set itself to work to get possession of Indian affairs, so that the treasury can be more successfully plundered." Philip H. Sheridan to William T. Sherman, February 28, 1870, Box 81, Philip H. Sheridan Papers, Library of Congress. For information on Vincent Colyer, and Grant's Peace Policy, see Robert H. Keller, Jr., *American Protestantism and United States Indian Policy, 1869–82* (Lincoln: University of Nebraska Press, 1983); Francis Paul Prucha, *American Indian Policy in Crisis: Christian Reformers and the Indian, 1865–1900* (Norman: University of Oklahoma Press, 1976); and Robert Winston Mardock, *The Reformers and the American Indian* (Columbia: University of Missouri Press, 1971). For the dispute between Sheridan and Colyer see Paul A. Hutton, "Phil Sheridan's Pyrrhic Victory: The Piegan Massacre, Army Politics, and the Transfer Debate," *Montana the Magazine of Western History*, 32 (Spring 1982): 32-43.

3. Red Cloud was chief of the Oglala Sioux and Spotted Tail was chief of the Brulé Sioux. They were no doubt in Davies' mind because of the successful war Red Cloud had recently waged in Wyoming, driving the army out of its forts in the Big Horn and Powder River country. The Fort Laramie Treaty, ending that conflict and establishing a Sioux reservation that included most of present South Dakota west of the Missouri River, had been ratified by Congress in February 1869. The treaty also granted the Sioux hunting rights along Nebraska's Republican River, in the same area that Sheridan's party planned to hunt. See James S. Olson, *Red Cloud and the Sioux Problem* (Lincoln: University of Nebraska Press, 1965); George E. Hyde, *Spotted Tail's Folk: A History of the Brulé Sioux* (Norman: University of Oklahoma Press, 1961); and George E. Hyde, *Red Cloud's Folk: A History of the Oglala Sioux Indians* (Norman: University of Oklahoma Press, 1937).

4. The superintendent of the Northwestern Railroad had placed the railroad director's private car at the disposal of Sheridan's party. At Omaha a similar courtesy was extended by the superintendent of the Union Pacific Railroad. On the return trip the Kansas Pacific Railroad did the same. *New York Times*, October 7, 1871.

The courtesy shown Sheridan by the various railroad executives is reflective of the close bond that existed between the frontier military establishment and the railroaders. Self-interest and past fellowship tied the two groups together. Most of the railroad construction bosses, surveyors, and engineers were former soldiers with close ties to the military establishment. Grenville M. Dodge, chief engineer of the Union Pacific, had commanded an army corps during General Sherman's Atlanta campaign. William J. Palmer, president of the Kansas Pacific, and W. W. Wright, superintendent of the same line, were both former Union army generals. These personal relationships naturally resulted in close cooperation between the soldiers and the railroadmen. Military escorts for surveying parties and construction crews were readily provided. Whole regiments were often transferred to provide more manpower to oblige the requests of the railroaders.

A tangible sign of the railroaders' gratitude was the liberal disbursement of valuable railroad passes to army officers. Sheridan held passes for several western and midwestern railroads, and private Pullman cars were often placed at his disposal when he traveled. Sheridan unhesitatingly requested extra passes for friends, even if the anticipated travel was purely for pleasure.

This alliance was only natural, considering the heavy federal investment in the western railroads. It was undoubtedly in the best interest of the government, the military, the capitalists, and the people to have the railroads completed as rapidly as possible, especially the transcontinental lines. These rail lines enabled the cheap and rapid transport of troops and supplies and eventually allowed the army to abandon many western forts. More importantly, from the military standpoint, the roads split the northern Indian tribes from the southern ones, spelled doom for the buffalo, and brought in more settlers.

For a listing of Sheridan's railroad passes see Forsyth Letterbooks, Box 45, Sheridan Papers. For the relationship between the military and the railroaders see Paul Andrew Hutton, *Phil Sheridan and His Army* (Lincoln: University of Nebraska Press, 1985), 169-79; Robert G. Athearn, *Union Pacific Country* (Lincoln: University of Nebraska Press, 1976), 209-10; O. M. Poe, "Report on Transcontinental Railways, 1883," in *Report of the Secretary of War [1883]*, 4 vols. (Washington, D.C.: Government Printing Office, 1883), 1: 253-317; Jerry M. Cooper, "The Army as Strikebreakers— The Railroad Strikes of 1877 and 1894," *Labor History*, 18 (Spring 1977): 179-96; and Stanley P. Hirshon, *Grenville M. Dodge: Soldier, Politician, Railroad Pioneer* (Bloomington: Indiana University Press, 1967).

5. Lawrence R. Jerome was one of the most prominent men in New York society. He was well known on both sides of the Atlantic for his business acumen, but it was his ready wit and reputation as a high-stakes gambler that made him famous. Among his close

17. *The Far West—Shooting Buffalo on the line of the Kansas Pacific Railroad* was the title for this drawing appearing in *Leslie's Illustrated Newspaper*, June 3, 1871. Such incidents remained common so long as the southern herd lingered near the rail line. Special trains were sometimes filled with amateur hunters who could slaughter the animals without ever leaving the comfort of their Pullman

friends were numbered Chester A. Arthur, Roscoe Conkling, Charles Delmonico, James Gordon Bennett, Jr., and the Prince of Wales. He was one of twelve children born to Isaac and Aurora Jerome, and he grew up on the family farm in the hill country near Pompey, in Onondaga County, New York. Although he first studied law with an uncle, Jerome soon turned away from Blackstone and toward business. Eventually he settled in Rochester and went into business with his older brother, Leonard. The Jerome brothers shared similar tastes in women as well as business, for they soon courted and married sisters. The brothers then purchased houses alongside each other and built a connecting passage so they would not have to go outside to visit. Their wives' inheritance enabled the Jerome brothers to purchase the *Rochester Daily American*, which became quite a successful Whig newspaper. Lawrence's work for the Whig party secured his first political job, when President Millard Fillmore appointed him Collector of the Port of Rochester.

The brothers sold the newspaper in 1850 and moved to New York City where they moved in with their older brother, Addison, and invested heavily in Wall Street. Despite an extravagant lifestyle, Lawrence made a fortune and retired from business to devote himself fully to politics, sports, and travel. In 1870 he was elected alderman and later made an unsuccessful bid for Congress. That defeat soured Jerome on politics, and for the rest of his life he simply played the role of the great wit, bon vivant, and man-about-town.

His eldest son, Lovell Hall Jerome, was a West Point graduate who served in the Second Cavalry from 1870 until he resigned in 1879. He was with the troops that hastily buried the victims of Custer's Last Stand on the Little Big Horn in 1876, and the following year he was awarded the Congressional Medal of Honor for gallantry in a charge against Chief Lame Deer's Miniconjou Sioux at Muddy Creek, Montana.

*New York Times*, August 13, 1888; Ralph G. Martin, *Jennie: The Life of Lady Randolph Churchill. The Romantic Years 1854–1895* (Englewood Cliffs, New Jersey: Prentice-Hall, 1969), 2-7, 17-18, 122, 265.

6. Leonard W. Jerome was even better known in New York society than his distinguished younger brother. He is best remembered today as the grandfather of Winston Churchill, but in the Gilded Age he was called the "King of Wall Street" and the "Father of the American Turf." He pursued financial fortune, women, and sport with equal amounts of skill and passion and was a great success at all three.

After being suspended from Princeton (then the College of New

Jersey), Leonard graduated from Union College in Schenectady, New York, and went to work for his uncle, Judge Hiram Jerome, a former law partner of Abraham Lincoln's. He married the black-eyed beauty Clara Hall in 1849, and her substantial inheritance allowed him to turn away from the law toward journalism and the financial world. After his successful operation of the *Rochester Daily American* with his brother Lawrence, he moved to New York City and, with his brother Addison and William Travers, formed a business partnership that quickly prospered. Jerome's speculative forays into Wall Street were legendary as he made great fortunes, lost them, and then made them again. The *New York Times* labeled him "one of the boldest, coolest, and most successful manipulators in Wall Street." When he retired from business in the 1870s he was worth millions.

During the Civil War, Jerome proved an active supporter of the Union cause. He served as treasurer of the Union Defense Committee and gave generously to various relief measures for veterans and their families. He contributed thirty-five thousand dollars toward the construction of the *Meteor*, a Union vessel designed to destroy the famed rebel raider, the *Alabama*. During the bloody 1863 New York City draft riots he manned a Gatling gun that defended the offices of the *New York Times*, of which he was part owner, from the rioters.

Along with August Belmont, the Rothschild agent in the United States, Jerome founded the American Jockey Club and made horse racing not only a respectable activity but also *the* social event of the time. He was also active in yachting, establishing the first international trans-Atlantic race. "People like Belmont and Jerome do not enter Society," noted one observer, "they create it as they go along."

Jerome's passion for sport was matched only by his keen interest in women. Actresses and singers were his great weakness, and he was particularly smitten by the "Swedish Nightingale," Jenny Lind. When his second daughter was born on January 9, 1854, he somehow persuaded his wife to name her Jennie. She grew to be a ravishing, strong-willed beauty who married Lord Randolph Churchill in 1874 and bore him a son, Winston, that same year.

Jerome had met General Sheridan in France during the Franco-Prussian War. The Grant administration had used Jerome as a diplomatic courier to Prince Otto von Bismarck, the brilliant strategist who had crushed Emperor Napoleon III's grandiose dreams at Sedan. Sheridan and Bismarck had become warm friends during the war when the American general accompanied the Prussian high command as an observer. Sheridan accompanied Jerome when he visited Bismarck at Versailles during the siege of Paris in February 1871.

Jerome died in Brighton, England, on March 3, 1891, at the age of seventy-three. His final illness had been a long and debilitating one, but, true to character, in his last days he ate only oysters and drank nothing but champagne. He was mourned in the highest social circles on both sides of the Atlantic. The body was brought back to America and was buried in the family mausoleum in Greenwood Cemetery, Brooklyn.

For Leonard Jerome's life see *New York Times*, March 5, 1891; Anita Leslie, *The Fabulous Mr. Jerome* (New York: Henry Holt, 1954); and Martin, *Jennie: The Life of Lady Randolph Churchill*. The society that Jerome was so important a part of is revealed in Allan Nevins and Milton Halsey Thomas, eds., *The Diary of George Templeton Strong*, 4 vols. (New York: Macmillan, 1952); Stephen Flake, *Offhand Portraits of Prominent People* (New York: Lockwood and Sons, 1884); Ward McAllister, *Society as I Have Found It* (London: Cassell, 1890); and Matthew Hale Smith, *Sunshine and Shadow in New York* (Hartford: J. B. Burr and Company, 1870). An interesting pictorial history is Allen Churchill, *The Upper Crust: An Informal History of New York's Highest Society* (Englewood Cliffs, New Jersey: Prentice-Hall, 1970).

7. James Gordon Bennett, Jr., ranks among the most important and influential, if not distinguished, newspapermen of American history. He was equally famous for his eccentricities, his madcap escapades in high society, and his devotion to yachting and horses.

His father, James Gordon Bennett, Sr., established the *New York Herald* on May 1, 1835, and revolutionized American journalism. He broke with the staid conventions of a profession more dedicated to offering opinion than to providing news. While other sheets reprinted Congressional speeches verbatim or reported the activities of European royalty, the *Herald* splattered every gory detail of the latest murder across its front page. By concentrating on local, rather than international, news, Bennett, Sr., attracted thousands of new readers. Many accused Bennett of pandering to the bad taste of the masses, but others viewed him as a Jacksonian savior for journalism, finally publishing news for all the people. Whatever the case, he made many enemies. Despite the immense wealth he accumulated, he was completely ostracized from New York society because his paper did not cater to the upper crust. In fact, he delighted in reporting their scandals, both personal and professional. His exposure of stock frauds on Wall Street infuriated the business community, as did his suggestion upon John Jacob Astor's death that half his fortune should be returned to the people of New York from whom he had stolen it. Bennett broke with the literary custom of referring to arms and legs as "branches of the body," to pants as "inexpressibles," to shirts as "linens," and to petticoats not at all, and thus brought down on his head the wrath of bluenoses, professional moralists, and bible thumpers of various persuasions. They viciously assailed him in print and pressured advertisers not to do business with the *Herald*. "Petticoats—petticoats—petticoats—" he thundered back at them in an 1840 editorial, "there, you fastidious fools, vent your mawkishness on that." The circulation of the *Herald* soared, reaching ninety thousand daily by 1867.

Bennett, Sr., paid a heavy price for success. When his son was born on May 10, 1841, the rival *New York Sun* insinuated that Bennett was not the father. In the resultant libel suit, the *Sun* lost. (The reference to the *New York Sun* on page thirteen of *Ten Days on the Plains* thus has special meaning.) When Bennett opposed the 1850 candidacy of John Graham for district attorney, he was attacked while strolling down Broadway with his wife by Graham and several goons carrying whips. They mercilessly beat him while two policemen idly watched. Two years later a bomb was delivered to his *Herald* office but was discovered before it went off. Mrs. Bennett fled to France with her children to escape the attacks, both physical and printed. The family was only reunited for short visits. Thus James, Jr., grew up away from the influence of his father.

The younger Bennett was raised in an atmosphere of indulgence and luxury in Paris, educated by private tutors. He returned to New York in his mid-teens and lived half of the year with his father. His imperious manner and command of the French language overwhelmed the genteel set who so despised his father. After all, anyone who could speak fluent French must be incredibly cultured—or so at least thought the New York upper crust of the 1850s. In 1857 Bennett, Jr., became the youngest member ever admitted to the New York Yacht Club (in 1871 he was elected Commodore). Along with the Union and Jockey clubs, it was the most exclusive organization in New York. His father purchased Junior the 160-ton yacht *Henrietta* to honor his new position in society.

When the Civil War broke out, Bennett, Jr., enlisted in the United States Navy. The *Herald* had long been identified with pro-southern and anti-Lincoln factions, but after Fort Sumter it rallied to the Union banner. The enlistment of young Bennett in the navy was further evidence of family loyalty to the Old Flag. The enlistment, however, was rather unusual, for this new third lieutenant in the Revenue Cutter Service came with his own ship, the *Henrietta*. In this manner Lieutenant Bennett avoided the distasteful duty of taking orders from social inferiors who might outrank him and also managed to reside shipboard in the manner he was accustomed. The *Henrietta*, armed with two six-pound rifled bronze guns and a twelve-pound brass cannon, boldly guarded the Long Island Sound from Confederate invaders throughout the summer of 1861. The prospects for action loomed larger when the *Henrietta* was ordered to join the blockading fleet off Port Royal, South Carolina, in February 1862. The old sea dogs in command of the Union blockade were not accustomed to the habits of New York yachtsmen and, having no desire to be educated, ordered the *Henrietta* decommissioned on April 29, 1862. Young Bennett, faced with the sour prospect of serving on another ship, resigned his commission on May 11, just a few days short of his first anniversary as a naval officer.

After two years of intensive apprenticeship with the *Herald*, Bennett, Jr., became managing editor in 1866 and two years later was named editor and publisher. The elder Bennett did not enjoy his retirement for long, dying on June 1, 1872.

Many expected this idle, wastrel youth to fail, but they did not count on his vigor and imagination, or on his determination to escape from his father's shadow. In the last decade of the elder Bennett's management, the *Herald* had actually become quite respectable, emerging as a major force in world journalism. Its Civil War coverage and European dispatches were the envy of its rivals. Bennett, Jr., determined to continue this reputation for excellence, moved the juicier news items to an afternoon edition, the *Evening Telegram*. Printed on pink paper, this penny-dreadful featured bold, eye-catching headlines that trumpeted stories on gruesome murders and salacious scandals, foreshadowing the tabloids of a later day. The *Evening Telegram* certainly paved the yellow-journalism road that Pulitzer and Hearst followed to fame and fortune.

While the *Evening Telegram* covered the sensational, the *Herald* continued to provide breakfast readers with outstanding local, national, and world coverage. Bennett continued the *Herald*'s reputation for war reportage. In 1867 he sent Henry M. Stanley to cover the British expedition against Abyssinia and the next year dispatched DeBenneville Randolph Keim to report General Sheridan's winter campaign against the Cheyenne Indians. The best-known war correspondent in the world, Aloysius MacGahan, who was a cousin of General Sheridan's, worked for the *Herald*. His coverage of the Franco-Prussian War, the Paris Commune, the 1873 Russian expedition against Khiva, and of his own remarkable adventures in Asia, sent the *Herald*'s circulation soaring. That tradition was still alive at the turn of the century when Richard Harding Davis, the best-known war correspondent of his era, reported the Boer side of the British war in South Africa.

Bennett determined not only to report the news but also to make it. MacGahan helped him do that through his Asian exploits, but the *Herald*'s greatest coup came in 1871 when Stanley found David Livingstone. The Scottish missionary-explorer had not been heard from in three years when Bennett ordered Stanley to find him in 1869. Stanley's epic African adventures were reported in the *Herald* in loving detail, including the triumphant moment on November 10, 1871, when he discovered Livingstone at Ujiji and uttered the now-famous phrase: "Dr. Livingstone, I presume?" Bennett financed several more African expeditions by Stanley, but as the reporter-explorer's fame grew, so did Bennett's jealousy. Eventually, he attempted to discredit Stanley, and their collaboration ended bitterly. The same sad ending came to Bennett's relationship with MacGahan.

Bennett financed other news-making enterprises, including the 1875 expedition of the bark *Pandora* to find a Northwest Passage and the tragic 1879–1881 expedition of George W. De Long to find the North Pole. De Long and several members of his party starved to death in Siberia after their ship was crushed by ice. But none of these expeditions ever rivaled Stanley's African adventure in capturing the world's attention. Such tactics attracted more readers to the *Herald*, which boasted a circulation of 190,500 in 1885.

Domineering, headstrong, and erratic, Bennett ran the *Herald* with an iron hand. Upon assuming the editorship at the tender age of twenty-five, he had informed his staff: "I want you fellows to remember that I am the only one to be pleased. If I want the *Herald* to be turned upside down, it must be turned upside down." Even after he moved to Paris in 1877, he cabled daily instructions to his New York editors, and no one could be hired or fired without his approval. Since editors tend to eventually acquire high opinions of themselves, some men grew weary of this. Once when Bennett ordered a reporter to meet him in Paris, the *Herald*'s editor refused to comply, claiming the man's services to be indispensable in New York. Bennett then asked for a list of those *Herald* employees who were considered indispensable. When he received the list containing twelve names, he fired them all. "I will have no indispensable men in my employ," he declared.

Bennett was equally famous as a sportsman on both sides of the

Atlantic. He introduced polo to the United States in 1876. Along with his close friend Leonard Jerome, he revived the sport of coaching in America. It was the rage in England at the time. Bennett, along with Jerome and August Belmont, organized the Coaching Club, and they could be seen, along with most society "swells," tooling along city streets and country byways dressed to the nines. Bennett, adding a new twist to coaching, would gallop his four horses down country roads at night sans clothing. Bennett also worked with Jerome and Belmont to found the Jockey Club in 1866.

It was not coaching or the turf, however, but yachting on which Bennett made the greatest mark. He initiated and participated in the first transatlantic yacht race in 1866. Bennett's *Henrietta*, with jolly Lawrence Jerome along as a passenger, won the race and the ninety-thousand-dollar prize, despite a gale that almost swamped all the contestants. In his later years Bennett offered prizes to encourage balloon, automobile, and airplane racing.

In 1877 Bennett left the United States amidst great scandal and took up residence in Paris, where he lived for the rest of his life. Two years earlier, Bennett, at thirty-five, had decided to settle down, being smitten by the winsome Caroline May, daughter of a prominent New York doctor. But the engagement was quickly broken off after the inebriated groom-to-be relieved himself—described at the time as "a breach of the most primitive of good manners"—in the drawing room fireplace of the May family before a large gathering of guests. Perhaps Bennett, who had after all been raised to know better, had simply decided that desperate measures were needed to save himself from the altar. It certainly worked. Soon after, Caroline's brother assaulted Bennett in front of the Union Club with a whip. John G. Heckscher managed to separate the combatants until another day. On January 7, 1876, Bennett and May, accompanied by numerous friends, doctors, and vitally interested spectators, met at Slaughter's Gap on the Maryland-Delaware border in the grandest sporting event of their lives—a duel. Fortunately, each duelist fired harmlessly into the air and then went off, arm in arm, to get roaring drunk together. New York society, however, was not as forgiving as Caroline May's brother. Although still welcome at the Union Club by the Jerome brothers and his other cronies, Bennett was shunned by the rest of high society. Enraged, Bennett moved to Paris, spending the rest of his days as an expatriate.

He did not marry until September 10, 1914, taking as his bride his longtime companion the Baroness de Reuter. Regarded as one of the most beautiful women in Europe, the Baroness, formerly Maud Potter of Philadelphia, had been widowed in 1909 by the death of Baron George de Reuter, whose family founded the famed British news agency. The fiesty, adventurous, scandalous journalist was thoroughly tamed and domesticated by his bride. She even got the world-famous pagan to join the Protestant Episcopal Church.

Bennett was absolutely devoted to the Baroness, and the marriage was a most happy one, although brief. On May 14, 1918, Bennett died from a massive brain hemorrhage at Beaulieu, France. After services at Trinity Church in Paris, he was buried at Passy. Soon after his death, the *New York Herald*, the *Evening Telegram*, and the *Paris Herald* (founded by Bennett in 1887) were sold to Frank Munsey for four million dollars. Eventually the *Herald* was absorbed into the *New York Herald Tribune*, and the last vestige of a great newspaper dynasty vanished.

For a well-written and entertaining biography of Bennett see Richard O'Connor, *The Scandalous Mr. Bennett* (Garden City, New York: Doubleday and Company, 1962). Also see Don C. Seitz, *The James Gordon Bennetts Father and Son: Proprietors of the New York Herald* (Indianapolis: Bobbs-Merrill Company, 1928); Albert Stevens Crockett, *When James Gordon Bennett Was Caliph of Bagdad* (New York: Funk & Wagnalls Company, 1926); Oswald Garrison Villard, *Some Newspapers and Newspaper-Men* (New York: Alfred A. Knopf, 1923), 273-81; and Steven D. Lyons, "James Gordon Bennett, Jr.," in Perry J. Ashley, ed., *American Newspaper Journalists, 1873–1900* (Detroit: Gale Research Company, 1983), 7-16.

8. Carroll Livingston had much in common with the Jerome brothers, being a prominent member of the New York Stock Exchange and an avid horseman. He was often a judge at horse exhibitions at Long Branch, New Jersey. He was born in 1833 in the New York town and county bearing his family name, and unlike the Jeromes and Bennetts, he possessed an impressive blue-blooded pedigree. He was a collateral descendant of Chancellor Robert R. Livingston of New York, who administered the oath of office to President George Washington in 1789. Livingston was educated in France, where he spent many of his early years, and at Harvard. In France he had established a reputation as an enthusiastic hunter. He died at his New York City residence on April 26, 1904, in his seventy-first year. *New York Times*, April 27, 1904.

9. John Gerard Heckscher, a prominent New York businessman, had served as an officer in the Twelfth Infantry during the Civil War.

10. Charles Lane Fitzhugh, although referred to by Davies as "an old officer of Gen. Sheridan's command during the war," was still quite young at the time of the buffalo hunt. Fitzhugh attended the United States Military Academy at West Point but resigned in 1861, two years before his class was to graduate, to fight in the Civil War. He received a commission as first lieutenant in the Fourth Artillery. Although first assigned to the western theater of conflict, where he was breveted captain for gallantry at the Battle of Shiloh, Fitzhugh spent most of the war fighting in the East. At Gettysburg Fitzhugh commanded one of the four batteries positioned near the clump of trees that marked the center point of Pickett's Charge. He participated in Sheridan's ten-thousand-man cavalry raid against Richmond in May 1864 as commander of a battery of horse artillery. In February 1865 Fitzhugh transferred to the cavalry as colonel of the Sixth New York Cavalry. In the final campaign leading to Lee's surrender at Appomattox, Fitzhugh commanded the second of three brigades in Thomas C. Devin's First Division of Sheridan's cavalry corps. Fitzhugh's brigade, consisting of the Sixth, Ninth, and Nineteenth New York Cavalry, and the Seventeenth and Twentieth Pennsylvania Cavalry, saw much hard fighting. Fitzhugh won another brevet for gallantry in this campaign at the Battle of Five Forks. On March 13, 1865, Fitzhugh was breveted brigadier general in both the volunteer and regular armies for gallantry and meritorious service. He resigned from the army on May 22, 1868, to pursue a business career, eventually becoming one of Pittsburgh's most prominent business leaders.

Brevets were honorary promotions for distinguished military service. Officers were often assigned to special commands and staff positions by brevet rank. When mixed units, such as cavalry and infantry or volunteer and regular commands, served together, brevet rank prevailed. Officers wore the insignia of their brevet rank and were addressed, both officially and socially, by their brevet rank. This caused considerable confusion on occasion, and so in 1869 and 1870 Congress passed regulations forbidding officers to wear brevet insignia or be addressed in official correspondence by brevet rank. Brevet rank could also no longer take precedence over regular army rank. Brevets continued to retain predominance in social relationships, however, and officers continued to be referred to by their brevet rank. As was the custom, Davies refers to all military officers in his book by their brevet rank.

For Fitzhugh's military career see Francis B. Heitman, *Historical Register and Dictionary of the United States Army*, 2 vols. (Washington, D.C.: Government Printing Office, 1903), 1: 423; Robert Underwood Johnson and Clarence Clough Buel, eds., *Battles and Leaders of the Civil War*, 4 vols. (New York: Thomas Yoseloff, 1956), 3: 374 & 4: 191, 714; L. Van Loan Naisawald, *Grape and Canister: The Story of the Field Artillery of the Army of the Potomac, 1861–1865* (New York: Oxford University Press, 1960), 295, 491; and Stephen Z. Starr, *The Union Cavalry in the Civil War: The War in the East from Gettysburg to Appomattox 1863–1865* (Baton Rouge: Louisiana State University Press, 1981), 200, 352, 366, 381, 428.

11. M. Edward Rogers was a Philadelphia businessman and noted philanthropist. For an account of the society of which he was a part see E. Digby Baltzell, *Philadelphia Gentlemen: The Making of a National Upper Class* (New York: Free Press, 1958).

12. John Schuyler Crosby, born in Albany, New York, on September 19, 1839, was descended from two of New York's most eminent families. His paternal great-great-grandfather was Colonel William Floyd, a signer of the Declaration of Independence, while on the maternal side he numbered Colonel Stephen J. Schuyler and General Philip Schuyler among his ancestors. In 1863 he married Harriet Van Rensselaer, who presented an equally impressive pedigree.

Crosby attended the University of the City of New York from 1855 to 1856, but left education behind to undertake a world tour. He ventured into China, the East Indies, and the Pacific Islands and participated in a daring crossing of South America from Santiago, Chile, to Buenos Aires on the Atlantic.

He returned to the United States at the outbreak of the war, enlisting as a lieutenant in the First Artillery. He first saw service in the Army of the Potomac, but in 1862 he was transferred to the Department of the Gulf. He served on the staffs of Generals Nathaniel P. Banks and Edward R. S. Canby. Staff duty did not keep Crosby out of combat, for he received three brevet promotions for gallantry in action and the personal thanks of President Abraham Lincoln for his heroism. By the end of the war, he ranked as a brevet lieutenant colonel in both regular and volunteer grades.

When Sheridan was ordered to the Rio Grande in May 1865 in a show of force against the French occupation of Mexico, Crosby joined his staff. He served Sheridan as aide-de-camp, with the rank of lieutenant colonel, from then until December 31, 1870. Crosby participated in Sheridan's 1868–1869 winter campaign against the Cheyennes and their allies. Upon Sheridan's 1869 promotion to lieutenant general, Crosby continued as his aide-de-camp on the staff of the Division of the Missouri. Staff duty in Chicago did not appeal to Crosby as had the adventurous days of Indian campaigning, and he resigned from the army on December 31, 1870. He and Sheridan, however, remained warm personal friends.

Since he had inherited considerable wealth, he could afford to devote the rest of his life to sport—shooting and yachting were his passions—and public service. From 1876 to 1882 he was American consul in Florence, Italy, and from 1882 to 1884 he served as governor of Montana Territory. As governor he assisted General Sheridan's efforts to protect Yellowstone National Park from commercial exploitation, accompanying President Chester A. Arthur and Sheridan on an inspection tour of the park in August 1883. Aided by Senator George Vest, Crosby and Sheridan blocked the efforts of the Northern Pacific Railroad to gain monopoly rights to key areas in the park and secured competent military protection for Yellowstone.

In 1903 Crosby became embroiled in the much-publicized controversy between Frederic Remington and Charles Schreyvogel. Remington, enraged over his competitor's success, criticized the accuracy of Schreyvogel's epic painting, *Custer's Demand*. The painting depicted a dramatic meeting that several hostile Indian chiefs had had with Custer and Crosby during the 1868 southern plains campaign. Crosby came to Schreyvogel's defense, vouching for the painting's accuracy and acidly noting that "doubtless Mr. Remington could have made a better picture, but doubtless he never did."

Crosby, long in ill health, died at Newport, Rhode Island, while on a yachting trip, on August 8, 1914.

Allen Johnson and Dumas Malone, eds., *Dictionary of American Biography*, 2 vols. (New York: Charles Scribner's Sons, 1927–1958), 2: 568-69; *New York Times*, August 9, 1914; Heitman, *Historical Register*, 1: 340; *The National Cyclopedia of American Biography*, 63 vols. (New York: James T. White and Company, 1891–1984), vol. 11; Hutton, *Phil Sheridan and His Army*, 84-86, 154, 354-60; Brian W. Dippie, "Frederic Remington's Wild West," *American Heritage*, XXVI (April 1975); R. C. Wilson, "The Great Custer Battle of 1903," *Mankind*, V (February 1976). Crosby contributed a chapter on his relationship with Sheridan to R. C. Greiner, *General Phil Sheridan as I Knew Him: Playmate-Comrade-Friend* (Chicago: J. S. Hyland and Company, 1908), 409-15.

13. Samuel Johnson's mansion on Chicago's Pine Street was a gathering place for that city's bachelors, including the Sheridan brothers. It was destroyed in the Great Chicago Fire of October 1871. Sheridan had already sponsored Johnson on a buffalo hunt-

ing trip to Fort Hays, Kansas, in September 1869. Lieutenant Colonel George A. Custer had entertained him that trip. Sheridan to Custer, September 25, 1869, Elizabeth B. Custer Collection, Custer Battlefield National Monument.

14. Anson Stager was one of General Sheridan's closest Chicago friends and often traveled west with him. He was a pioneer in the expansion of the telegraph and in the use of electricity.

Born in New York state on April 20, 1825, he was educated in the public schools and at the age of sixteen became a printer's devil in the *Rochester Daily Advertiser* office of Henry O'Reilly. When O'Reilly, working along with Samuel F. B. Morse, constructed a telegraph line from Philadelphia to Cincinnati, Stager transferred out of printing and into the telegraph office. He quickly rose from telegraph operator in 1846 to general superintendent of the Western Union Telegraph Company in 1856. He combined keen management skills with imaginative technical ability, being responsible for originating the system whereby telegraph wires could be worked from a common battery on a closed circuit. Stager also originated the cunning contract by which Western Union received the monopoly-right to string telegraph wires along major railroad routes.

After the attack on Fort Sumter, Stager was asked to take charge of the United States military telegraphs. He was appointed captain of volunteers and assistant quartermaster general on November 11, 1861, but with increasing responsibilities he was promoted to colonel and assigned as aide-de-camp to Major General Henry W. Halleck in Washington, D.C. Stager developed the Union military telegraph cipher system used throughout the war. For meritorious service he was breveted brigadier general of volunteers on March 13, 1865, and was mustered out of the volunteer army on September 1, 1866.

The Western Union Telegraph Company was reorganized after the war, divided into the Central, Eastern, and Southern Divisions. Stager was appointed superintendent of the Central Division, headquartered after 1869 in Chicago. Eventually he became a vice-president of the company.

New technology fascinated Stager, and he was active in the expansion of the telephone and electric light in Chicago and the West. He was one of the founders of the Western Electric Manufacturing Company, serving for a time as its president. From the time of its founding until his death, Stager served as president of the Western Edison Electric Light Company. He died on March 26, 1885, in Chicago. Heitman, *Historical Register*, 1: 914; Johnson and Malone, eds., *Dictionary of American Biography*, 9: 492-93; *Army and Navy Journal*, March 28, 1885.

15. Charles L. Wilson, owner and editor of the *Chicago Evening Journal*, the oldest daily in the Old Northwest, was born and educated in Fairfield County, Connecticut. He moved to Chicago in 1835, finding employment as a clerk in a mercantile store. His brother, Richard L. Wilson, established the *Evening Journal* in 1844 as a Whig campaign paper advocating the election of Henry Clay as president. Charles worked for his brother in the paper's editorial department, and when Richard Wilson was appointed postmaster by President Zachary Taylor in 1848, Charles moved up to the editorship.

As long as the Whig Party survived, Wilson remained its champion, and upon its demise he battled the nativist Know-Nothing Party that briefly threatened to replace the Whigs as a national party. In 1854 Wilson joined with other prominent Illinois Whigs, most notably Abraham Lincoln and Elihu B. Washburne, to form the Illinois Republican Party. At the Republican state convention in 1858, Wilson nominated Lincoln as the party's candidate to oppose Stephen A. Douglas for the United States Senate. During that losing campaign Wilson served as one of Lincoln's advisors.

In the contest for the Republican presidential nomination in 1860, Wilson was a strong advocate of his old friend, William H. Seward. When the nomination went to Lincoln, Wilson aggressively worked to unite the party behind the candidate. Upon Lincoln's election, Wilson was appointed secretary of the London Legation, a post he held for just over three years until July 1864.

Although he had conducted much of the *Evening Journal*'s business from London, Wilson now resigned his post in order to devote more attention to the paper as well as to work for Lincoln's reelection. The newspaper prospered after the war, and in 1872 Wilson had a five-story building constructed to house its operations. Under Wilson's direction the *Chicago Evening Journal* became one of the most influential and prosperous dailies in the country.

*Biographical Sketches of the Leading Men of Chicago* (Chicago: Wilson, Pierce, & Company, 1876).

16. Colonel Daniel H. Rucker served as assistant quartermaster general from 1866 until 1882, headquartered first in Philadelphia and then in Chicago. He was born on April 28, 1812, in Belleville, New Jersey, and as a youth resettled near Detroit, Michigan. He joined the army in 1837, winning a commission as second lieutenant of the First Dragoons. During the Mexican War Rucker was breveted for gallantry at the Battle of Buena Vista. After the war

Rucker, now a captain and brevet major, transferred from the line to the staff and served thereafter in the Quartermaster's Department. During the Civil War he ably assisted the quartermaster general, Montgomery C. Meigs, and was partially responsible for the high level of efficiency of the department. He emerged from the war as a brevet major general in both the volunteer and regular armies.

His daughter, Irene, married General Sheridan on June 3, 1875. His son, John A. Rucker, served as a lieutenant with the Sixth Cavalry on the frontier and drowned while on duty on July 11, 1878.

General Sheridan used his influence to force the retirement of Quartermaster General Meigs in February 1882 to make way for the promotion of his father-in-law. This act of nepotism caused quite a controversy since Meigs was five years younger than Rucker, quite healthy, and doing an excellent job. Rucker served as quartermaster general for only ten days before he also retired on February 23, 1882. He made his home in Washington, D.C., for the rest of his life, dying on January 6, 1910, just a little over three months short of his ninety-eighth birthday. See Ezra J. Warner, *Generals in Blue: Lives of the Union Commanders* (Baton Rouge: Louisiana State University Press, 1964), 414-15; Heitman, *Historical Register*, 1: 849; Russell F. Weigley, *Quartermaster General of the Union Army: A Biography of M. C. Meigs* (New York: Columbia University Press, 1959), 356-57; Hutton, *Phil Sheridan and His Army*, 141-42.

Dr. Morris Joseph Asch joined the army as an assistant surgeon on August 5, 1861. He was breveted major for service during the war. He served as General Sheridan's staff physician throughout the southern plains Indian campaigns and was a warm personal friend of the general's. It was Asch, along with Lieutenant Colonel Michael V. Sheridan, the general's younger brother who served as aide-de-camp on his staff, who completed all the advance work of organizing the buffalo hunt. Asch resigned from the army on March 31, 1873, and eventually became a rather prominent New York physician. He died on October 5, 1902. See Heitman, *Historical Register*, 1: 173; and Hutton, *Phil Sheridan and His Army*, 108, 154, 207, 213-14.

17. These are the two engraved cups pictured at the beginning of *Ten Days on the Plains*. The photographs of the cups, as were all the illustrations in the volume, were original *cartes de visite* pasted into each copy of the book. The buffalo cup was won by Charles Lane Fitzhugh and the elk cup by Charles Wilson.

18. Colonel (Brevet Major General) William H. Emory, commander of the Fifth Cavalry and the District of the Republican, Department of the Platte, was an old comrade-in-arms of Sheridan's from the Shenandoah Valley campaign. A Marylander, born in Queen Annes County on September 7, 1811, Emory graduated from West Point in 1831. His best friend at the military academy was Jefferson Davis, future president of the Confederacy. He served with the Fourth Artillery for five years after graduation but then resigned his commission to accept an appointment as a civil engineer with the Department of War.

Reappointed to the army as a first lieutenant in the Topographical Engineers in 1838, Emory distinguished himself in the 1844–1846 boundary survey between the United States and Canada. With the outbreak of war with Mexico, Emory was assigned as chief engineer officer for Brigadier General Stephen Watts Kearny's Army of the West. As part of Kearny's invasion of New Mexico and California, Emory surveyed the Gila River route to California. His talents, however, extended far beyond mapmaking, and he repeatedly distinguished himself during Kearny's California campaign, especially as commander of a squadron of dragoons at the Battle of San Pasqual. Emory received the brevets of captain and major for gallantry at San Pasqual and San Gabriel, California.

After the War Emory conducted the boundary survey between Mexico and the United States, completing this work in 1857. His reports on this survey, especially *Notes of a Military Reconnaissance from Fort Leavenworth in Missouri, to San Diego in California*, quickly became classic accounts of military exploration. So pleased was the government with this work that Emory was breveted lieutenant colonel and promoted to major in the Fifth Cavalry.

At the time of the attack on Fort Sumter, Emory was stationed in the Indian Territory (present Oklahoma). Despite his southern heritage he spurned offers of a Confederate command and was the only officer in rebel territory who extracted his troops without losing a man. Promoted to brigadier general of volunteers in March 1862, he participated in both the eastern and western theaters of conflict. In the 1864 Shenandoah campaign he commanded the Nineteenth Corps of Sheridan's army and was breveted up to major general of volunteers for his actions at Fisher's Hill and Cedar Creek. When Sheridan pushed south to rejoin Grant's forces for the final assault on Lee's army, he left Emory in command of the remaining Union forces in the Shenandoah. When mustered out of the volunteer army on January 15, 1866, Emory held the rank of major general, as well as brevets of major general in both the vol-

18. Colonel (Brevet Major General) William H. Emory.

unteer and regular armies. His permanent rank in the regular army was colonel.

After serving with his regiment on the frontier from 1869 to 1871, he was assigned to command of the Department of the Gulf (the states of Louisiana, Mississippi, and Arkansas) in November 1871, with headquarters at New Orleans. This was a difficult assignment, for the region was wracked by civil strife. The Ku Klux Klan and the White League used intimidation and violence to keep black citizens from voting, and the Republican government in Louisiana could survive only with military protection. Elections were a sham, with violence and fraud the rule.

President Grant ordered General Sheridan to inspect conditions in the Department of the Gulf in January 1875 and take command if he felt it necessary. Sheridan was determined to hold Louisiana in the Republican fold but found Emory "not at any time on the side of the Government." He characterized the colonel as a "very weak old man, entirely unfitted for this place," and in order to bypass him Sheridan annexed the department to his Division of the Missouri on January 4, 1875. Emory was relieved of his command of the department two months later and placed on waiting orders.

Emory retired on July 1, 1876, with the rank of brigadier general, after forty-three years of military service. He made his home in Washington, D.C., dying there on December 1, 1887.

George F. Price, *Across the Continent with the Fifth Cavalry* (New York: Antiquarian Press, 1959), 210-23; Warner, *Generals in Blue*, 142-43; Joseph G. Dawson III, *Army Generals and Reconstruction: Louisiana, 1862–1877* (Baton Rouge: Louisiana State University Press, 1982), 112-215; Hutton, *Phil Sheridan and His Army*, 264-65; William H. Goetzmann, *Army Exploration in the American West 1803–1863* (New Haven: Yale University Press, 1959), 127-44, 195-208.

19. Captain (Brevet Major) William H. Brown was born in 1837. He enlisted as a private in the Second Cavalry in 1858 and by the time of the outbreak of the Civil War had risen to the rank of sergeant. He received a commission in the Eleventh Infantry but soon resigned it to accept an appointment as second lieutenant in the Fifth Cavalry in October 1861. During the war he served as chief quartermaster for the regiment, attaining the rank of captain and the brevet of major.

Transferred to the frontier in September 1868, he saw hard service in Sheridan's 1868–1869 southern plains campaign. After relatively quiet garrison duty at Fort McPherson during 1870–1871, he led the first detachment of the Fifth Cavalry that was transferred to Arizona. He was actively engaged in the Tonto Apache campaign of 1872–1873, being thrice recommended for brevet promotions for gallantry in action against the Apaches. During 1873–1874 he commanded Camp Grant and the San Carlos Apache Reservation. In June 1874 he applied for a sick leave, dying on June 4, 1875, in New York City.

Price, *Across the Continent with the Fifth Cavalry*, 403-4; Heitman, *Historical Register*, 1: 254.

20. Major (Brevet Major General) Eugene A. Carr ranked as one of Phil Sheridan's premier frontier combat officers. There was hardly an officer in the army with more experience fighting Indians.

Born in Erie County, New York, on March 20, 1830, Carr entered West Point at the age of sixteen. He graduated in July 1850 and was assigned to the Regiment of Mounted Riflemen. He received severe wounds in an 1854 fight with Mescalero Apaches in Texas and was promoted to first lieutenant in recognition of gallantry in action. He saw more hard service in the Sioux expedition of 1855, the Kansas border troubles of 1856–1857, the Utah expedition of 1857–1858, and campaigns against the Kiowas and Comanches in 1859–1860.

Carr's Civil War career was no less distinguished. Appointed colonel of the Third Illinois Cavalry in August 1861, he soon rose to command the Fourth Division of the Army of the Southwest. At the battle of Elkhorn Tavern in 1862, he was thrice wounded while holding the Union line at a critical juncture in the campaign leading to the important Battle of Pea Ridge. He was awarded the Congressional Medal of Honor for gallantry at Elkhorn Tavern. After recovering from his wounds, he commanded a division of cavalry in the western theater of conflict throughout the rest of the war, winning brevets up to major general in both the volunteer and regular armies.

With full Cossack beard and erect military bearing, Carr inspired confidence in those around him and, as Phil Sheridan once noted, was "always active, competent and brave." When Sheridan organized his 1868–1869 winter campaign against the Cheyennes, he specifically requested Carr's services. Sheridan's confidence was not displaced, for Carr and his Fifth Cavalry troopers brought the campaign to a rousing conclusion with a smashing victory over the notoriously hostile Cheyenne Dog Soldiers at the Battle of Summit Springs, Colorado, on July 11, 1869. Tall Bull, the leader of the Dog Soldiers, was slain by scout Bill Cody. The power of the Cheyenne war faction was broken by Carr's victory at Summit Springs.

With Colonel Emory often on detached service, it was Carr who commanded the Fifth Cavalry and made that regiment one of the finest on the frontier. He participated in the Great Sioux War of 1876–1877, joining in the actions at Warbonnet Creek and Slim Buttes.

In 1879 he was promoted to colonel and assigned to command the

19. Major (Brevet Major General) Eugene A. Carr.

Sixth Cavalry. He led that regiment in campaigns against the Apaches in Arizona and New Mexico in the 1880s and in the Sioux campaign of 1890–1891.

Promoted to brigadier general on July 19, 1892, he retired from the army six months later. He made his home in Washington, D.C., in his last years, dying on December 2, 1910. He is buried at West Point.

For an excellent account of Carr's career see James T. King, *War Eagle: A Life of General Eugene A. Carr* (Lincoln: University of Nebraska Press, 1963).

21. Fort McPherson was established on September 18, 1863, on the south side of the Platte River, some twenty miles from North Platte, Nebraska. The post was first called Cantonment McKean, then Fort Cottonwood, and finally, in 1866, Fort McPherson. By the time of the 1871 hunt, it was a fine post, with quarters for five companies built of cedar, and with extensive stables and storehouses. The post was abandoned in April 1880.

*Outline Description of the Military Posts in the Division of the Missouri* (Fort Collins, Colo.: Old Army Press, 1972), 70-73; Francis Paul Prucha, *A Guide to the Military Posts of the United States 1789–1895* (Madison: State Historical Society of Wisconsin, 1964), 89.

22. There has been a considerable amount of recent scholarship on the lives of women on the military frontier. See Sandra L. Myres, "Romance and Reality on the American Frontier: Views of Army Wives," *Western Historical Quarterly*, XIII (October 1982): 409-27; and Patricia Y. Stallard, *Glittering Misery: Dependents of the Indian Fighting Army* (Fort Collins, Colo.: Old Army Press, 1978). A bibliography of writings by and about frontier army wives, compiled by Sandra L. Myres, is included as an appendix to Teresa Griffin Vielé, *Following the Drum: A Glimpse of Frontier Life* (Lincoln: University of Nebraska Press, 1984), 157-73.

23. Lieutenant (Brevet Major) Edward M. Hayes served as quartermaster for both the 1871 hunt and the Grand Duke Alexis hunt in 1872. A New Yorker, he had enlisted as a youth in the Second Cavalry in 1855 and was involved in several sharp Indian fights on the Texas frontier. He returned home to attend school upon the expiration of his enlistment in 1860 but promptly reenlisted upon the outbreak of the Civil War.

In January 1863 Hayes was appointed a first lieutenant in the Tenth Ohio Cavalry, then a part of the Army of the Cumberland. During the final two years of the war, Hayes served as a captain and aide-de-camp for Brigadier General Judson Kilpatrick, participating in many of the cavalry actions that marked General William T. Sherman's campaign against Atlanta and his subsequent march to the sea. Hayes was made a brevet major of volunteers for gallantry during the campaigns in Georgia and the Carolinas on

20. Fort McPherson, Nebraska, as it appeared in 1873. The officers' club, store, and post saloon are in the foreground.

March 13, 1865, and was mustered out of the volunteer army on July 24, 1865.

In the post-war army reorganization, Hayes was appointed a second lieutenant in the Fifth Cavalry on February 23, 1866. After serving on Reconstruction duty in North Carolina, Hayes was transferred to the frontier where he served as a battalion quartermaster throughout General Sheridan's 1868–1869 southern plains campaign. He was appointed regimental quartermaster on June 22, 1869, and served in that capacity until he accompanied Colonel Emory to New Orleans as aide-de-camp in 1872.

After Emory was replaced as commander of the Department of the Gulf, Hayes was transferred back to his regiment and also promoted to captain. He served with the Fifth throughout the Great

21. Captain Edward M. Hayes and H Company, Fifth Cavalry, form the escort for President Chester A. Arthur's 1883 visit to Yellowstone National Park.

Sioux War, participating in the 1876 skirmishes at Warbonnet Creek and Slim Buttes.

After several staff appointments in the East, Hayes was stationed at Fort Washakie, Wyoming, as commander of H Company, Fifth Cavalry. In the summer of 1883 General Sheridan personally selected Captain Hayes and his company to provide the military escort for President Chester A. Arthur's excursion to Yellowstone National Park.

In 1893 Hayes was promoted to major and transferred to the Seventh Cavalry, where he served until his appointment as lieutenant colonel, Fourth Cavalry, in 1899. He became colonel of the Thirteenth Cavalry in 1901 and retired two years later, on January 26, 1903, eleven days after his promotion to brigadier general.

Price, *Across the Continent with the Fifth Cavalry*, 446-49; Heitman, *Historical Register*, 1: 515.

24. Davies is referring to Ned Buntline's serial, "Buffalo Bill, the King of Border Men," which ran in the *New York Weekly* beginning December 23, 1869, and to Fred G. Maeder's 1871 dramatization of Buntline's story. The play carried the same title as the serial story.

25. This is a misprint. Davies means General Emory.

26. Charles Wilson, reporting back to his newspaper, the *Chicago Evening Journal*, shared Davies' estimation of Cody, describing him as "the observed of all observors—splendid in form, the beau ideal of the rough rider that he is. . . ." *New York Times*, October 7, 1871.

Cody's appearance was carefully planned beforehand. "I rose fresh and eager for the trip," he later wrote, "and as it was a nobby and high-toned outfit which I was to accompany, I determined to put on a little style myself. So I dressed in a new suit of light buckskin, trimmed along the seams with fringes of the same material; and I put on a crimson shirt handsomely ornamented on the bosom, while on my head I wore a broad *sombrero*. . . . I felt firstrate that morning, and looked well." William F. Cody, *The Life of Hon. William F. Cody Known as Buffalo Bill* (Lincoln: University of Nebraska Press, 1978), 282.

27. Davies of course means General and Mrs. Emory. Mrs. Emory, the former Matilda Wilkins Bache, was the great-granddaughter of Benjamin Franklin.

28. These camps were decidedly unusual for the frontier. Cody later described them thus:

> Our camps were constructed with great care. Three of the
> twenty-five wagons in our train were travelling icehouses,
> to keep the game and wine cold. The wagons were parked

22. William F. Cody, circa 1880.

in a square at night, the mules and horses being picketed inside the square, which was several acres in extent. The soldiers lay at each end of this camp. . . .

There were none of the discomforts of roughing it upon that expedition. A course dinner of the most delicious viands was served every evening by waiters in evening dress and prepared by French cooks brought from New York. The linen, china, glass, and porcelain had been provided with equal care, and a big woodfire lent cheerfulness to the dining-tent. This was floored and carpeted with much care, and for years afterward travellers and settlers recognized the sites upon which these camps had been constructed by the quantities of empty bottles which remained behind to mark them.

Buffalo Bill [William F. Cody], "Famous Hunting Parties of the Plains," *Cosmopolitan*, XVII (June 1894): 139-40. In his autobiography Cody closely follows the account of the hunt in Davies' book, often simply paraphrasing it. In his 1894 *Cosmopolitan* article, however, he presents an entirely original version of the hunt.

29. Although the 1867 Treaty of Medicine Lodge had established reservations for the Cheyennes, Arapahos, Kiowas, Comanches, and Kiowa-Apaches in the Indian Territory (Oklahoma), the Indians, for the most part, had failed to settle on their new lands. Congress, preoccupied with the impeachment of President Andrew Johnson, also failed to appropriate funds to fulfill the government promises of food, clothing, doctors, and teachers until July 1868. By then it was too late to prevent hostilities with the disgruntled and still undefeated Indians.

The Cheyennes, in particular, were not interested in peace. With the 1864 Sand Creek Massacre still fresh in their minds, the Cheyennes were naturally hesitant about placing themselves under the government's protection and control. In June 1868 a party of Cheyennes raided their traditional enemies, the Kaws, in Kansas, and two months later a large raiding party attacked the white settlements along the Saline and Solomon Rivers in Kansas, killing fifteen men and raping five women. General Sheridan, commanding the Department of the Missouri (embracing the Indian Territory, Kansas, Missouri, Colorado, and New Mexico), sent two of his most trusted scouts, William Comstock and Abner Grover, to meet with the Cheyennes and discuss their grievances. Near a Cheyenne village on the Solomon River, Comstock was killed and Grover was seriously wounded by a Cheyenne war party.

None of this surprised Sheridan, who felt the peace to have been tenuous at best. To Sheridan's mind the only way to ensure a lasting peace was to see the Cheyennes "soundly whipped, and the ringleaders in the present trouble hung, their ponies killed, and such destruction of their property as well will make them very poor."

Sheridan now ordered the Cheyennes and Arapahos to report to their reservations in Indian Territory and to surrender the leaders of the Kansas raids as stipulated in the Medicine Lodge Treaty. This the Indians refused to do, and so all the Cheyennes and Arapahos were branded as hostiles. The Comanches, Kiowas, and Kiowa-Apaches, who had taken no part in the Kansas raids even though they often raided the Texas settlements to the south, were considered friendly and were promised sanctuary on their Indian Territory reservations.

Realizing that he had too few soldiers to mount much of a summer offensive, Sheridan concentrated on protecting the line of the Kansas Pacific Railroad. He did recruit fifty frontiersmen to be used as a ranger detachment against the Indians. Commanded by Sheridan's aide, Major George A. Forsyth, these scouts confronted a large party of Cheyennes under Roman Nose and Tall Bull on Colorado's Arickaree Fork of the Republican River in September 1868. Surprised by hundreds of warriors, the scouts were besieged on a small island in the Arickaree for nine days before a rescue column of the Tenth Cavalry saved them. In the battle Forsyth was shot three times and gravely wounded; his second in command, Lieutenant Fred Beecher, was killed, as was the doctor and five of the scouts. Nineteen other scouts were wounded. They had, however, put up a stiff defense, killing Roman Nose and a large number of his warriors. Nevertheless, the Battle of Beecher's Island disabused Sheridan of using such small detachments for offensive operations.

In hopes of pulling the hostiles down out of Kansas, Sheridan next sent Lieutenant Colonel Alfred Sully, with eight companies of cavalry and another of infantry, south across the Arkansas River to attack the families of the Cheyennes and Arapahos reportedly camped along the Cimarron River in Indian Territory. Although Sully skirmished with the Indians, he moved too slowly to close with them and returned to Fort Dodge on September 18, 1868, in failure.

Within the boundaries of Sheridan's command, since the Kansas raids of early August, 110 civilians had been killed, thirteen women raped, over a thousand head of stock stolen, farms, stage buildings and wagons burned, and all travel halted on the major roads. Eighteen of Sheridan's troopers had been killed and forty-five wounded, with little damage inflicted upon the hostiles. Western political and business interests demanded action. The army, which had emerged from the Civil War with a self-image as one of the world's great modern armies, was humiliated by its inability to handle a few thousand poorly armed nomadic natives.

Sheridan determined on a winter campaign to crush the hostiles. Although campaigning against Indians in winter was not a new idea, Sheridan's campaign was universally viewed as a bold, innovative plan. Sheridan was convinced that his well-fed-and-clothed soldiers could challenge the severe climate long enough to strike a decisive blow. Winter would limit the Indians' mobility, which was their greatest advantage. Their ponies would be weakened by scarce fodder, while the Indians themselves would seek the comfort of their teepees, lulled into a false sense of security by the weather. Distance and climate had always protected them from their enemies in winter. But the railroad had ended that advantage, for supplies could now be shipped to distant depots, giving the soldiers greater mobility.

Sheridan planned for several columns to converge on the country of the Cheyennes and Arapahos. Major Andrew W. Evans would lead over five hundred men eastward from Fort Bascom, New Mexico, to scour the Canadian River region of the Texas Panhandle for Indians. Major Eugene A. Carr was to march south from Fort Lyon, Colorado, with seven companies of his Fifth Cavalry, to be joined on the North Canadian by five more companies of cavalry already in the field under Captain William Penrose, and proceed toward the Antelope Hills in search of Indians. Sheridan did not expect these columns to do much damage to the Indians but hoped they might drive the hostiles toward the Antelope Hills. When Sheridan's main column from Fort Dodge attacked the Indians in the Antelope Hills, the troops under Carr and Evans would block any escape to the west or north.

The central strike force was commanded by Sheridan and consisted of eleven companies of the Seventh Cavalry under Lieutenant Colonel George A. Custer, the Nineteenth Kansas Volunteer Cavalry under Colonel Samuel J. Crawford, who had resigned as governor of Kansas to lead the new volunteer regiment, and five companies of infantry under Captain J. H. Page.

First blood was drawn by Custer, who struck Black Kettle's Cheyenne village on the Washita River in Indian Territory on November 27, 1868. Custer claimed to have slain 103 warriors, while capturing fifty-three women and children. Among the dead was Black Kettle, the leading peace chief among the Cheyennes. De-

23. Phil Sheridan sat with several of his officers in the Topeka, Kansas, photographic studio of J. Lee Knight in January 1872. Left to right: Lieutenant Colonel George A. Custer, Lieutenant Colonel George A. Forsyth, Lieutenant General Philip H. Sheridan, Major Morris J. Asch, Major Nelson B. Sweitzer, Lieutenant Colonel Michael V. Sheridan, Lieutenant Colonel James W. Forsyth.

spite the peaceful reputation of Black Kettle, the camp contained army mules, letters taken from murdered army couriers, and photographs captured in the Kansas raids. It was, however, a costly victory, with two officers and nineteen enlisted men killed and fourteen others wounded.

A month later, on Christmas Day, Major Evans struck a Kiowa and Comanche village at Soldier Spring, due south of the Washita battlefield, and routed the inhabitants. Although he inflicted few casualties on the Indians, Evans did destroy large quantities of food and camp items. Most of the Kiowas and Comanches who had not already gone onto their Indian Territory reservation did so now.

After establishing a major post, Fort Sill, to guard the new Indian reservations, Sheridan sent Custer, with the Seventh and the Nineteenth Kansas, westward into the Texas Panhandle in search of the remaining Cheyennes and Arapahos who had not surrendered. On March 25, 1869, Custer located a large Cheyenne village on Sweetwater Creek, just west of the Texas line. The Cheyennes held two white women as captives, so Custer chose to negotiate rather than attack. In a parley Custer seized three Cheyennes as hostages and forced the Indians to turn over the women. He then promised to release the three hostages, as well as his Washita prisoners, if the Cheyennes would surrender. The Indians agreed to this, and Custer, short on rations, hurried back to his supply base in Indian Territory.

Most of the Cheyenne and Arapaho bands surrendered in the spring of 1869, but the most belligerent of the Cheyennes, Tall Bull's Dog Soldiers, moved north to join the Sioux. To counter the Dog Soldier threat, Sheridan transferred Carr and the Fifth from Fort Lyon, where they were recuperating from the winter campaign, to Fort McPherson, Nebraska. The Fifth arrived none too soon, for the Dog Soldiers and their Sioux allies soon raided the line of the Kansas Pacific Railroad and the settlements along the Republican River and its tributaries.

Carr, with eight companies of the Fifth and three companies of Pawnee Indian scouts, pursued the raiders for a month, finally surprising Tall Bull's village on July 11, 1869, at Summit Springs in northeastern Colorado. In a fierce engagement, the Cheyennes were routed, their eighty-four lodges and all other property destroyed, and fifty-two Indians killed and another seventeen captured. One white woman captive was rescued, although another was murdered before the troops could save her. Tall Bull, the leader of the Cheyenne war faction, was slain by scout Bill Cody.

The Battle of Summit Springs climaxed Sheridan's 1868–1869 campaign and broke the power of the Cheyennes. Although some of the other Dog Soldier bands escaped north into Wyoming, most returned to the Indian Territory to surrender. Sheridan had achieved the three major goals of his campaign: removing the Indians from the land between the Platte and Arkansas rivers and securing the safety of the railroads and settlers; punishing the Indians involved in the Kansas raids; and forcing the southern plains tribes onto their reservations. Although a success, the campaign was not decisive. The Red River War of 1874–1875 completed the subjugation of the southern plains tribes.

For Sheridan's 1868–1869 campaign see Hutton, *Phil Sheridan and His Army*, 28-114; Robert M. Utley, *Frontier Regulars: The*

*United States Army and the Indian 1866–1891* (New York: Macmillan, 1973), 142-62; William H. Leckie, *The Military Conquest of the Southern Plains* (Norman: University of Oklahoma Press, 1963), 88-132; Stan Hoig, *The Battle of the Washita: The Sheridan-Custer Indian Campaign of 1867–69* (Garden City: Doubleday & Co., 1976); John M. Carroll, ed., *General Custer and the Battle of the Washita: The Federal View* (Bryan, Tex.: Guidon Press, 1978); Charles J. Brill, *Conquest of the Southern Plains: Uncensored Narrative of the Battle of the Washita and Custer's Southern Campaign* (Oklahoma City: Golden Saga Publishers, 1938); and DeBenneville Randolph Keim, *Sheridan's Troopers on the Borders: A Winter Campaign on the Plains* (Lincoln: University of Nebraska Press, 1985).

30. Cody knew these buffalo hunters quite well, as their camp had been set up on Medicine Creek, about twenty miles south of Fort McPherson, for some time. They were John Y. Nelson, Hank and Monte Clifford, Arthur Ruff, and Dick Seymour.

Nelson, in particular, was a well-known figure around North Platte and Fort McPherson and ranked as one of the most knowledgeable men in the region regarding the Sioux. His wife was a relative of the great Oglala chief, Red Cloud. Nelson, a Virginian who had come west as a fur trader, was also an adopted member of Spotted Tail's Brulé Sioux. His Sioux name was Cha-Sha-Cha-Opoyeo, which means Red-Willow-Fill-the-Pipe. Nelson had helped guide Brigham Young's Mormon party to Utah in 1847 and had often served the army as a scout. His command of the Sioux language and influence with the Indians led the government to often employ him during negotiations and treaty councils. When Cody began to tour on the eastern theater circuit, he took Nelson with him. Later, when the Wild West was organized, Nelson served as an Indian interpreter, cowboy, and assistant to Cody in his marksmanship displays. Nelson was best known, however, as the driver of the Deadwood stage. With full, flowing white beard he established a visual stereotype later copied on the motion picture screen by actors such as Gabby Hayes and Al St. John. Cody once described his old friend as "a good fellow, though as a liar he has but few equals and no superior."

Cody, *Life of Hon. William F. Cody*, 272, 285; Nellie Snyder Yost, *Buffalo Bill: His Family, Friends, Fame, Failures, and Fortunes* (Chicago: Swallow Press, 1979), 37-38, 128; Don Russell, *The Lives and Legends of Buffalo Bill* (Norman: University of Oklahoma Press, 1960), 308.

24. This buffalo hunters' camp, photographed by Robert Benecke in 1874 near Sheridan, Kansas, is probably similar to the camp on Medicine Creek that Sheridan's party visited in 1871.

31. Cody, in his *Cosmopolitan* article, gives a bit more detail on how Jerome acquired Buckskin Joe.

Larry Jerome gave an amusing illustration, on this hunt, of that great appreciation of practical jokes which in after-years afforded so much amusement to his cronies. When the party was fitting out, each of the gentlemen from New York asked me if I would get him a good buffalo horse. Of course, I had never seen any of them before, and I was equally anxious to please them all. I noticed from the first, however, that Mr. Larry Jerome made a special point of cultivating me, and, after a number of civilities on his part, it cropped out that he wanted to ride Buckskin Joe, a horse of my own, whose exploits were famous all over that country. I discovered how the wind set even before he made his request, and cheerfully consented to it. "Now," said Jerome, "don't you say a word to any of the others about my having a horse, and I'll have some fun with them."

So, for the next day or two, Mr. Jerome would go about with a long face and announce, in a melancholy way, that he much feared that he would not be able to find an appropriate mount; he didn't think he could find a horse that would carry him, anyway, as he was a heavy man; and so on. The morning we started, he disappeared from view, and in a few moments dashed into the party, equipped cap-a-pie, on Buckskin Joe, with my own saddle, bridle, and rifle. Joe jumped and cavorted, and Mr. Jerome was in his glory.

But the hour of retribution was at hand. Buckskin Joe had been trained to chase the buffalo at full speed and lay his rider alongside of the biggest animal he could find in the herd. The first herd we started for, Jerome rode away full of spirits, and Buckskin Joe, as if determined to do all that was expected of him, took the bit in his mouth, left the rest of us far in the rear, and picked out the ugliest-looking bull, a creature of really gigantic size, for Mr. Jerome's special delectation. As Buckskin Joe got within a few feet of this monster, Jerome dropped his rifle, and, after much endeavor, persuaded his charger to stop and, dismounted to pick up his gun, when he was horrified to see Buckskin Joe dash away after the herd, leaving him afoot on the prairie. He got no game and was with due solemnity court-martialed that night in camp for los-

25. *Great Royal Buffalo Hunt*, by Louis Maurer. Painted in 1894, this is the second version of the hunt done by Maurer.

ing his horse. He made an extremely witty speech in his own defense and said that it was evidently Buckskin Joe's hunt a great deal more than his own; but he was found guilty and sentenced to eat seven smoking buffalo cutlets in rapid succession, a penalty he paid with much cheerfulness.

Cody, "Famous Hunting Parties of the Plains," 138-39.

32. It is interesting to note that Davies seems unimpressed by the loyalty and courage of the prairie wolf, or coyote, who returned to fight and perish with his mate. As such, he reflects an ancient prejudice against wolves that is ably discussed in Barry Holstun Lopez, *Of Wolves and Men* (New York: Charles Scribner's Sons, 1978).

33. In his *Cosmopolitan* article, Cody identifies the culprits in the Indian raid. "At our last camp, on the Saline river, an Indian scare was gotten up for Mr. Jerome's benefit. Mr. Crosby, Mr. Hecksher [*sic*], and some others of the younger members of the party, disguised themselves as Indians and sneaked into the tents, with a result of much laughable confusion."

Cody, "Famous Hunting Parties of the Plains," 139.

34. Fort Hays, Kansas, was established on October 18, 1865, to protect the construction crews for the Kansas Pacific Railroad. The original site of the post, on the Big Creek branch of the Smoky Hill River, was abandoned because of flooding in 1867. The fort was relocated about a quarter mile from Big Creek, and about a half mile from Hays City and the railroad.

It was a well-established post in 1871, with quarters for four hundred men. Most of the post buildings were of frame construction with shingle roofs. With the Indian threat over, the army abandoned Fort Hays on November 8, 1889.

*Outline Description of the Military Posts*, 127-30; Prucha, *Guide to the Military Posts*, 78.

35. The news that reached the hunters was of the October 2, 1871, issuance of an arrest warrant for A. Oakley Hall, mayor of New York City and henchman of the notorious "ring" of "Boss" William Marcy Tweed, for malfeasance in office. Although Hall was never convicted, it was the beginning of the rapid fall of Tweed's political machine. Both Lawrence Jerome and Henry Davies had had political battles with Tweed in the past.

36. The Great Chicago Fire began on Sunday evening October 8, 1871, sweeping north and east from Halsted and Twelfth streets, whipped by dry, thirty-mile-an-hour winds. A three-and-a-half-square-mile area of Chicago was destroyed, with property losses

26. Fort Hays, Kansas, in 1873, showing enlisted men's barracks and the mess hall.

later estimated at $200,000,000. At least 250 were killed, and over 100,000 were homeless as a result of the fire. Among the buildings destroyed was Sheridan's headquarters. He lost all of his personal and professional papers. On October 9, Sheridan took charge of the city to insure order as well as to distribute relief.

Hutton, *Phil Sheridan and His Army*, 209-12.

# INDEX

Page numbers in parentheses refer to illustrations.

Utah War, 28, 154

Van Rensselaer, Harriet, 146
Vest, George, 147

Wales, Prince of, 137
Warbonnet Creek, Battle of, 38, 41,
  154, 159
Ward, Artemus, 70
Washburne, Elihu B., 149
Washington, George, 144
Western Edison Electric Light Com-
  pany, 148
Western Electric Manufacturing Com-
  pany, 148
*Western Literary Journal*, 23
Western Union Telegraph Co., 66, 148
Whig Party, 149

White League, 153
Wild West show, 35, 41-45
Wilson, Charles L., 22, 149, 150, 159;
  on 1871 hunting trip, 66, 99, 104-5.
  (87)
Wilson, J. G., 6
Wilson, James H. (5)
Wilson, Richard L., 149
Winchester, Battle of, 8
wolves, 109-11, 170
women, on the military frontier, 156
Wright, W. W., 135

Yellow Hair, 38, 40-41, 45
Yellowstone National Park, 16n.12, 17,
  147, 159
Yellowstone River, 38
Yellow Tavern, Battle of, 8
Young, Brigham, 28, 166